The ALL-NEW
complete
pregnancy
cookbook

The ALL-NEW complete pregnancy cookbook

FIONA WILCOCK
MSc, PGCE, BA, RPHNutr

CARROLL & BROWN LIMITED

*This book is dedicated to my mother, Marie Smith,
who taught me so much about cooking and who died whilst
I was writing this edition.*

First published in 2013 in the
United Kingdom by

Carroll & Brown Limited
20 Lonsdale Road London NW6 6RD

Art Director Chrissie Lloyd
Managing Art Editor Emily Breen
Photography Jules Selmes, David Murray
Home Economist Clare Lewis
IT Management John Casey

Printed in China

CONTENTS

INTRODUCTION

Pregnancy will be a very exciting time in your life, as a new person comes into being and grows inside you. It is also a time of huge emotional upheaval as you plan for the future, sometimes feeling anxious and worried, sometimes feeling euphoric but there will be time for reflection as well, as you consider the moments that have passed, and look forward to a child-oriented life.

Pregnancy can also be a time of mixed health; you may feel overwhelmingly tired and suffer from complaints you have never experienced, or you can look more lovely and feel sexier than you ever have done before.

Bound up with this whole physical and emotional experience is your diet. The nutrients you eat during pregnancy supply your baby with the essential building blocks for life and a have a significant effect on your child's long term health. Eating well is also vital in maintaining your own health and well-being, right from the time you think about having a baby through to after your baby is born. Food provides the nutrients and energy you'll need to get on with your everyday life – sometimes helping to ease common complaints – but it is also a source of pleasure, as an occasional indulgent treat or a delicious dinner with family and friends.

The recipes in this book have been devised with all this in mind, as they contain the key nutrients you need to support pregnancy and breastfeeding. By checking the nutritional analysis pages, you'll easily be able to find recipes, which, for example, provide 25% or more of your daily needs for folic acid, iron or vitamin C, even when cooking losses have been taken into account.

To make it even simpler, I've written and nutritionally analysed weekly menu plans for each of the three trimesters and one for the newborn weeks. These allow you to choose from a range of different recipes for breakfast lunch and dinner, and feel confident that your nutritional requirements will be met.

HOW TO USE THIS BOOK

The **All–New Complete Pregnancy Cookbook** provides you with the dietary information, meal plans and recipes that will optimise both your nutrition and your enjoyment of food during your pregnancy.

Chapter One is about eating well in pregnancy, and you'll find this chapter particularly useful in understanding why you and your baby depend upon specific nutrients.

Chapter Two focuses on the foods which help you achieve your pregnancy needs, providing lots of suggestions and information on the different food groups.

Chapter Three is about feeling good in pregnancy, maintaining a healthy weight, making safe food choices and using foods to deal with common pregnancy complaints.

Chapter Four contains detailed menu plans taking you through the three trimesters to the early newborn weeks and breastfeeding. The recipe suggestions in italics are those that you can find in the book, but I also include easily prepared or bought dishes. The menu plans ensure that you'll meet more than 90% of your requirements for all the major vitamins and minerals (*) throughout your pregnancy and whilst breastfeeding.

The **RECIPES** chapter contains over 100 double-tested recipes designed to maximise your nutrition and to suit how you feel at various stages in your pregnancy. They are simple to make, allowing you to spend less time in the kitchen, and if you are not an experienced cook, there are simple instructions and tips to guide you. As well as substandtial dishes for breakfast, lunch and dinner, I've included a range of 'little bites' for when you are not feeling overly hungry and one-pot recipes, for when you want to make as little mess in the kitchen as possible. Most of the recipes will serve two, but can often be doubled if you have visitors or are feeding other children, and many can be frozen. Each recipe contains preparation and cooking times and if applicable, serving suggestions, storage and allergen information.
   Although the introduction will give you some idea of the essential nutrients each dish contains, there is a complete nutritional profile for each recipe at the back of the book.

*except vitamin D which should be taken as a 10mcg supplement,

CHAPTER 1

EATING WELL

This chapter explores what makes up a healthy pregnancy diet and how you can ensure you benefit from one. If you are already eating healthily, you may just have to make a few minor adjustments or, if you know that your diet really isn't as good as it should be, you will want to take a more critical look at what you eat. Increasingly we hear about the long-term consequences of eating well in pregnancy on a baby's future health (see box), so use this opportunity to find out more about a great diet, remembering it is never too early OR too late to improve the quality of what you eat.

Not yet pregnant?

It is always best to plan ahead, so if you haven't yet conceived, being in tiptop health will help. Trying to be the right weight for your height is a critical starting point (see page 29).

Apart from your pre-pregnancy weight, eating well before conceiving is important, as pregnancy places demands on your body's stores of many minerals and vitamins and may quickly deplete them. So an ideal pre-pregnancy diet is rich in key nutrients such as iron, calcium, iodine, magnesium and zinc and important vitamins especially folic acid and vitamin D. You can find out why these are important by looking at the later section in this chapter, and can make dishes, which are rich in these nutrients, by referring to the nutritional analysis of the recipes on page 154.

Because of their isoflavone content, which act like oestrogens, soya beans may affect sperm concentrations, so if your partner is a great consumer of soya products, it may be worth him cutting them out if you are trying for a baby.

Birth weight and your baby's health

Research suggests that babies who are born small and undernourished are at greater risk of developing diabetes, high blood pressure and heart disease in later life. There are many reasons why some babies are born with a low birth weight – not all of which you can control – but there are some lifestyle factors you can change to enable your baby to achieve her full potential:

- *Avoid alcohol, smoking and drug-taking before you conceive and during pregnancy;*
- *Don't restrict eating a healthy diet for fear of weight gain, especially if you entered pregnancy underweight, or don't regularly eat a healthy balance of foods.*

Large birth weight babies can also suffer complications such as respiratory problems and jaundice; women who suffer from pregnancy diabetes are more at risk of having larger babies.

Having twins or more?

Women carrying more than one baby require extra nutrients and additional calories to support the added increase in blood volume and uterine size as well as the development of two or more babies. In particular, this means an increased need for calcium, iron and essential fatty acids, especially omega 3 fatty acids.

If you're having twins (or more babies) your diet needs to contain a great mix of nutrient-rich foods. In addition to the 400 mcg of folic acid and 10 mcg of vitamin D, which are recommended for all pregnant women, you should consider taking (or may be prescribed) a prenatal supplement that provides zinc, magnesium, calcium, vitamin B_6, vitamin C, vitamin E and iron. DHA (a fatty acid) is also important, so look out for a supplement, which contain 300 mg DHA without vitamin A (retinol).

THE KEY NUTRIENTS

Protein

Vital to every body cell, your baby needs you to eat protein-rich foods so that she can grow and develop normally. You also need protein to make the extra red blood cells required for your greatly increased blood volume.

Protein is made up of chains of amino acids — some of which your body can make while others must be found in foods. The latter are the essential amino acids, which are found almost exclusively in animal-based foods such as meat, poultry, fish and dairy products. Strict vegetarians, however, can ensure they have the right balance of amino acids by planning their diet carefully to include tofu and soya beans as well as other pulses, seeds and grains.

Carbohydrates

The main source of dietary energy, carbohydrates are easily broken down by the body to supply glucose. However, it's important to try to eat carbohydrate-rich foods that have been minimally processed as these are likely to provide a more sustained release of glucose into the blood stream rather than a peak followed by a trough, which may increase the risk of developing pregnancy diabetes. Put very simply, it is a case of eating more wholegrain foods (and lower GI foods) and minimising your use of sugars and sweetened drinks.

Good-quality carbohydrates are important so a low carbohydrate, high protein diet is not suitable for pregnancy.

Fats

The amount of fat in your diet shouldn't increase in pregnancy, but you may need to pay attention to the quality of the fats you are eating to ensure your baby receives sufficient essential fatty acids. As with your pre-pregnancy diet, you should be keeping your intake of saturates down by using oils and spreads high in monounsaturates rather than saturates-rich butter, ghee or animal-based spreads or frying fats. However you do still need fat in your diet so, in addition to oils, you should include nuts and seeds, which supply essential fatty acids, and avoid processed foods that supply partially hydrogenated (trans) fatty acids.

Essential fatty acids

These are the fatty acids that the body can't generate itself so are needed in your diet. Commonly referred to as omega 3 fatty acids, alpha linolenic acid (ALA) is the most abundant in foods, and the body can convert this, to a limited degree to DHA (docosahexanoic acid) and EPA (eicosapentaenoic acid). These are the two very long chain omega 3 fatty acids that are vital for your baby's growth and development.

DHA is very important as it plays a key role in the development and maturation of your baby's brain and eyes. The richest supply of DHA is oily fish, and one important project on maternal and infant nutrition recommended that all pregnant women should have a minimum of 200mg of DHA a day, and eat fish at least once or twice a week, including oily fish such as salmon, herring and mackerel (See also page 32).

If you don't eat fish, you need to eat plenty of linseed, omega 3 fortified eggs and milk and green leafy vegetables. You can also look out for specially formulated supplements of DHA/EPA designed for use in pregnancy.

Fibre

There are two types, soluble and insoluble and it's the latter's ability to keep things moving through your digestive system that is especially important during pregnancy.

Soluble fibre is broken down in the bowel and serves a number of bodily roles but in pregnancy, it is its ability to help with satiety – keeping you feeling fuller – that can be useful if you are tempted to snack unhealthily. It is found in oats, peas, bean and lentils and fruit such as oranges, apples and pears.

Insoluble fibre, because it is not broken down, helps prevent constipation by keeping waste moving through the gut. Constipation can be a particularly trying issue at this time, as pregnancy hormones affect the speed at which waste goes through your gut. This type of fibre is found in wholegrain cereals, fruits, vegetables and seeds.

MINERALS

Calcium

This is essential for the proper growth and development of your baby's bones and teeth (your baby's first and adult teeth are present at birth!) as well as a healthy heart, muscles and nervous system.

If you didn't eat calcium-rich foods before you became pregnant, your bone stores of calcium may be low, and this increases your risk of calcium deficiency. It is known that there is a link between poor calcium intake and pre-eclampsia — a serious medical condition that occurs only in pregnancy. However, calcium supplements of up to 1g a day, can ensure that even women whose diet is very low in calcium are less likely to have pre-eclampsia or pre-term deliveries.

In the last trimester, your baby lays down a lot of bone and if you don't have adequate calcium in your diet, she will take it from your bones, leaving you more at risk from osteoporosis in later life. Your post pregnancy need for calcium also increases considerably when breastfeeding (see page 41).

Calcium works in conjunction with vitamin D (see page 16).

Potassium and sodium

Both of these are essential for all-round health and are found in all body cells and fluids including blood and lymph. Having the correct balance of fluids, especially in your blood, is crucial to your health. Salt is made up of sodium and another chemical called chloride. Too much salt is known to increase your blood pressure, which increases your risk of high blood pressure (hypertension) in pregnancy.

One way of controlling your blood pressure is to increase the amount of potassium you eat. Potassium-rich foods include many fruits and vegetables and wholegrain cereals, so a healthy diet where you have a minimum of five portions of fruit and vegetables a day will certainly help provide plenty of it.

In the past, pregnant women were sometimes advised to limit their salt intake to prevent the risk of pre-eclampsia but there is little evidence that this is effective. However, if you regularly eat a lot salty foods, cut down the amount of salt you use at the table and in cooking food before you become pregnant and don't increase it whilst you are pregnant.

minerals

Magnesium

Another pregnancy essential, magnesium has a huge number of functions in your body pregnant or not. These range from making protein and DNA for cells and tissues, ensuring the correct functioning of the nervous system to the more commonly understood role in bone formation. Magnesium is also involved in glucose and insulin metabolism ensuring your blood sugar levels are kept constant.

Conditions such as cerebral palsy, sudden infant death syndrome and mental retardation may be linked to a magnesium deficiency, and a substantial number of women, especially younger women in the UK do not have sufficient magnesium.

Like calcium, magnesium is stored in your bones, so if your diet is poor for some time, you will start to deplete your stores. There is also some evidence that low levels of magnesium are linked to leg cramps and pre-eclampsia. Good sources include pumpkin, melon and sunflower seeds; milk, bread, potatoes and leafy green vegetables.

Iron...

One in five women in the UK have inadequate iron in their diets. Therefore, around 20% of women are likely to enter pregnancy with low iron stores, and thus an increased risk of suffering from anaemia. If you have heavy periods, don't eat iron-rich foods such as meat or have a rather ad hoc vegetarian diet, you are at greater risk of iron deficiency. Have a look at the recipes (see page 154), which provide iron and eat more of them or take a multivitamin and mineral supplement when you are planning a pregnancy.

Iron

Iron is essential for the manufacture of blood cells and your blood volume increases rapidly in pregnancy. Your growing placenta also uses iron, and it has been estimated that around 680 mg of iron are needed to meet your baby's growth need, which comes from any stored iron as well as your diet.

How much iron you need in pregnancy is hotly debated; in the UK, it is thought that because a pregnant woman has improved efficiency in absorbing iron from foods and is no longer losing blood each month, the requirements don't actually increase. In fact, the further into pregnancy you go, the more efficient your body becomes at absorbing iron. However many women don't have sufficient iron in their diet whilst pregnant or before conceiving, meaning they are less likely to have iron tucked away to call on when their needs increase. Women are more likely to have low iron stores if:
- The pregnancy is unplanned;
- They've had a baby within the last eighteen months;
- They don't eat red meat such as beef or lamb, or other iron-rich foods;
- They are still teenagers.

Having low iron stores increases your risk of developing iron deficiency anaemia and although your baby will preferentially take iron from you, there is more chance he will be born underweight.

Developing iron deficiency anaemia in early pregnancy increases your risk of having a smaller placenta, which, in turn, can influence the size and health of your baby.

Becoming anaemic in your second trimester can increase your risk of giving birth prematurely and also of having a low birth-weight baby. Recent studies have also found that by tracking populations now in their fifties, there is a link between iron deficiency anaemia in the last trimester of pregnancy and schizophrenia in later life.

When breastfeeding, your milk supplies iron to your baby and your ability to absorb iron from food increases further so that your baby get's sufficient. However by around six months, breast milk alone does not meet your baby's need for iron.

Zinc

Surveys show that many women in the UK do not have sufficient dietary zinc and are actually zinc deficient. It is also known that women who enter pregnancy with low zinc stores are at an increased risk of having a preterm baby. So it's important to consider this important nutrient when planning your diet, including zinc-rich sources such as red meat, wholegrain cereals, beans and lentils.

Pre-conceptually, zinc is as important for men as women as it is an essential component of sperm.

Zinc and iron act antagonistically so if you are prescribed iron supplements, you may need to increase your zinc intake, too, or take a multi-mineral tablet, which provides both. As with calcium, your requirements only increase when you have had your baby and are breastfeeding, but unlike calcium can be harder to meet your requirements for zinc.

Copper

The role of this little-known nutrient is becoming better established and in pregnancy it seems to be important for your baby's brain development, particularly in the last few months of pregnancy. It also has a role in forming connective tissues in your baby's developing heart and immune system. Your need for copper does not increase in pregnancy, but if you are breastfeeding you need to eat plenty of copper-rich foods such as nuts, lentils and shellfish.

Selenium

This is an important antioxidant, which helps in many reactions in your body to protect you against cell damage, boosting your immune system in particular. As your body undergoes many complex changes during pregnancy, having adequate antioxidants is essential and low levels of selenium in the diet have been associated with an increased risk of developing pre-eclampsia. The selenium content of a diet depends on the soil in which foods are grown and where animals graze. It is thought that selenium intake in the UK is generally falling as we import less grain, especially wheat, from North America and Canada where the soil is richer in selenium. Good sources include fish, lentils and sunflower seeds.

Iodine

Iodine is vital because it is a component of the thyroid hormones, which regulate your metabolism. A severe lack of iodine in the diet pre-conceptually and during pregnancy can lead to fetal brain damage, or cretinism, a developmental condition, which, thankfully is rare in developed countries.

In the UK, iodine deficiency is relatively uncommon as iodine is found in milk, our main dietary source, which is drunk by a high proportion of the population. In addition fish, shellfish and seaweeds contain it. However, women who avoid milk or milk products and seafood, may not have sufficient dietary iodine. Vegan mums to be, therefore, are recommended to have a daily supplement even if they are taking seaweed because the amount varies (see also page 32). A supplement of 140 mcg started pre-conceptually and running throughout pregnancy would meet your needs.

VITAMINS

Vitamin A

Critical in pregnancy as it helps with the growth of all cells, vitamin A is essential for the development of your baby's organs, particularly eyes, and circulatory, respiratory and nervous systems. Vitamin A is also important for your immune system helping you fight disease and infection, as well as maintaining your vision. However, too much vitamin A can be dangerous, resulting in fetal malformations.

Vitamin A covers both retinol, which is found in animal foods, and carotenes, which are found in plant foods. The most commonly found carotene is beta carotene, which the body converts to retinol (the preferred source). Liver, which is a very rich source of retinol should not be eaten in pregnancy, nor should supplements that contain cod liver oil; these, too, contain too much retinol.

Thiamin

Also known as Vitamin B1, this plays an important role in releasing energy from food; your requirements only increase in the last trimester and when you are breastfeeding. It is commonly found in peas, brown rice, and green vegetables and pork is an exceptionally good source.

Riboflavin

Also known as vitamin B_2, this also has a role in energy release, and your requirements increase throughout pregnancy and further when breastfeeding.

Dairy foods are a great source of this vitamin and many of the recipes provide it. If you don't eat dairy foods, consider a pregnancy dietary supplement and ensure you eat fortified foods such as breakfast cereals or enriched soya drinks.

Niacin

Also known as vitamin B_3, this is also important to help release energy from food but additional quantities are not needed until you are breastfeeding. Like the other B vitamins, little is stored in the body so it is important to have a regular dietary supply. Niacin is found in meat and fish, especially turkey and haddock, in cereals, and also in nuts.

Some studies have suggested that adequate niacin along with vitamins B_6 and B_1 can help prevent cleft palate, and similar defects.

Vitamin B_6

Also known as pyridoxine, it can be depleted with the long-term use of the contraceptive pill and is not readily stored in the body, so having a pregnancy diet rich in this nutrient is important. Pork, fish, wholegrains, bread, eggs and potatoes are good sources. Your baby needs it for the normal development of his central nervous system and brain. It is also an important antioxidant protecting your cells against damage and helping your immune defences.

Vitamin B_{12}

This plays a crucial role in making red blood cells and genetic material. Vitamin B_{12} and folic acid both help convert a potentially harmful substance called homocysteine into a less harmful compound. This is important as high levels of homocysteine in the body increase the risk of circulatory diseases and nervous system diseases, which can affect you, and increase the risk of birth defects, especially neural tube defects, and result in premature birth and a low birth weight for your baby.

Vitamin B_{12} is only found in animal foods or algae, meaning that strict vegetarians need to ensure a

supply from a supplement or fortified foods. Long-term ovo-lacto vegetarians have been found to have lower levels of vitamin B_{12} in their blood which can predispose them to a deficiency in pregnancy, and a risk later on that their breast milk may supply inadequate amounts of B_{12} to their babies.

Folate

Or folic acid (the synthetic form) as it is more usually known to women, is an essential nutrient as it is well known to help reduce the risk of having a baby with neural tube defects (NTD). It also has other roles as described with B_{12} above. Having a supplement of 400 micrograms a day from before conception to the twelfth week of pregnancy is essential. If you previously had a baby with a NTD, this should be increased to 4 mg and if you are diabetic, 5 mg. Insufficient folate in pregnancy also can increase your risk of preterm delivery.

Folate in foods is very susceptible to destruction, so it is important that food sources, of which the highest are vegetables, are carefully prepared and cooked to minimise loss.

Good sources are green leafy vegetables, especially Brussels sprouts and broccoli, asparagus, beetroot, oranges, wholegrains and black eye beans.

Vitamin C

Perhaps the best known of the antioxidant vitamins, vitamin C or ascorbic acid plays an important role in protecting cells against damage, keeping your immune system working correctly and for the proper development and functioning of the placenta. Ascorbic acid helps the gut absorb iron from food, so is an essential part of a pregnancy diet, especially as only tiny quantities can be stored in the body.

Vitamin C is found in many fruits and vegetables but some can be lost through poor storage and cooking methods. Choose a quick cooking method

with minimum water such as steaming or microwave cooking, and cut items into large pieces to minimise losses through oxidation.

Vitamin D

This is essential for the body to effectively use calcium, and because it is found in very few foods, a supplement of 10 mcg a day is recommended in pregnancy and breastfeeding. Actually, most vitamin D is made by the action of sunlight on skin but you can't rely on sunshine to generate sufficient and, in fact, in winter, vitamin D is not synthesised in the UK.

In the UK, many women go into pregnancy with very low stores of vitamin D because of the following:

- Season: In the winter, due to lack of sun, we don't make any vitamin D.
- Latitude: The further away from the equator you live, the less vitamin D you can make; Scottish women have less chance to make it than women who live in southern England, for example.
- Skin pigmentation: If you have black skin you make less than if you have white skin.
- Cultural practices: Eating a vegan diet or covering the skin so preventing exposure to sunlight will result in low levels.
- Fear of sun exposure: If high-factor sunscreens are used to decrease the risk of skin cancer.

If you become pregnant with very low levels of stored vitamin D and don't take supplements, this may increase your risk of developing pre-eclampsia and pregnancy diabetes. There is also the possibility of longer term consequences such your baby's bones being poorly mineralised in early childhood, which in turn leads to rickets. There is also some evidence that persistent wheezing in childhood may be linked to poor vitamin D status in pregnancy. Obviously, adequate vitamin D whilst breastfeeding helps ensure your baby's bones can form properly, and that when he starts to walk they are strong enough to support him and ward off rickets.

Vitamin E

A group of form compounds called tocopherols form Vitamin E and they are important protective antioxidants. There is some evidence that low intakes of vitamin E are linked to an increased risk of pre-eclampsia. In the UK, there is no recommended daily amount for vitamin E as it is widely distributed in foods, and is carried into the body like other fat soluble vitamins in dietary fats and oils. Other countries recommend between 7 and 15 mg a day in pregnancy.

THE EATWELL PLATE

Fruit and vegetables

Starchy foods

Protein foods

Milk and dairy foods

Fatty and sugary foods

The four main food groups
Together, these should take up about 95% of your plate at all meals and you'll be assured of getting the most nutrients if you eat a variety of items from the different groups.

Starchy foods   Milk and dairy foods   Fruit and vegetables   Protein foods

Vitamin K

This fat soluble vitamin is essential for blood clotting and routinely given to newborn babies to prevent a rare haemorrhaging disease. There are no specific recommendations for this in pregnancy or breastfeeding in the UK, but ensuring that you eat green vegetables will provide a good supply.

A HEALTHY PREGNANCY DIET

The four main food groups

Whether pregnant or not, a balanced diet comprises eating a mixture of foods from four of the food groups illustrated by the 'Eatwell plate' . Each of these groups contains a wide range of foods, which supply a host of different nutrients, and you should aim to eat the relative proportions of them, which the plate suggests. The fifth group, which supplies foods high in fat and sugar, needs to be eaten in limited amounts as these foods supply few valuable nutrients, and tend to be very easy ones in which to over indulge! See below.

Starchy foods

Bread, rice, potatoes, pasta and cereals are among the foods rich in carbohydrates, which supply energy and B group vitamins. Make sure that at every meal, you fill at least a third of your plate with these types of foods. Choose wholegrain versions or brown rice for additional fibre and other nutritional benefits. Look out for fortified bread and breakfast cereals.

Fruit and vegetables

Whether fresh, frozen, dried or canned (in water or juice), these contain a wide range of vitamins, minerals and phytochemicals essential for a healthy pregnancy. Ensure you have a minimum of five portions every day (not counting potatoes), which should cover between a third and half your plate, and eat a variety of different colours and types to obtain all the different nutrients and protective substances. Bear in mind that fruit or vegetable juices count as only one portion.

Milk and dairy foods

As well as milk, yogurt, cheese and fromage frais, this group includes vegetarian sources such as soya milk and 'yogurts'. (Butter, cream and eggs are not dairy foods). These foods provide protein as well as calcium, B group vitamins especially B_{12} and B_2. Make sure you have three portions or the equivalent a day and choose reduced fat versions as they provide less fat, calories and saturates. If you can't or don't eat dairy foods, have calcium from other sources. Fortified soya milk and yogurts are a great alternative, and canned fish such as sardines and pilchards contain lots of calcium if you eat the bones.

Protein-rich foods

Meat, poultry, fish, eggs, beans, lentils and nuts are major sources of protein, as well as supplying key minerals such as iron, zinc, and magnesium (see detail on page 11). Fish contain iodine and oily fish omega 3 fatty acids (see page 24) and lentils, chickpeas, beans, seeds and nuts contain zinc, calcium, magnesium, selenium and iron.

Eat a high protein source at two meals a day. If you don't eat meat, poultry or fish, make sure you eat pulses, tofu, quorn as well as eggs and cheese to obtain dietary essentials without having too many saturates.

Fatty and sugary foods and drinks

Biscuits, cakes, crisps, ice creams, fizzy drinks, chocolate, etc., offer variety, interest and palatability to your diet but they are really extras not essentials. They are very energy dense — that is they contain high levels of fat and sugar in a small volume and usually provide few useful vitamins and minerals.

Oils, whether olive, rapeseed, corn or sunflower are around 99 per cent pure fat and whilst they provide some fatty acids the body can convert to omega 3 fatty acids, be careful not to have too much.

Many types of butter and fat spreads are available with reduced levels of fat, saturates and calories so choose these over the full fat versions. Have spreads rich in monounsaturates, such as olive spread.

CHAPTER 2

YOUR KEY FOODS

This chapter looks at individual foods and food groupings to highlight their specific nutrient value and to provide guidelines on what and how much to eat and any special care you need to be taking.

Grains and potatoes

These two items and the products made from them such as pasta, bread and some breakfast cereals are a healthy source of energy as they are high in carbohydrates and usually low in fat. They should provide between 45 and 60 per cent of the energy (calories) you eat. Low carbohydrate diets, which limit this food group, are not suitable during pregnancy.

The quality of the carbohydrate you eat is important and eating whole-grain or brown varieties of pasta, bread, cereals or grains improves the quality as more nutrients are provided.

'Whole grain' refers to the grain after the removal of inedible parts, but must include the entire germ, endosperm and bran. Whole grains include brown and wild rice, whole meal flour and products made from it such as bread and pasta, and whole grains of pot barley, maize, millet, buckwheat, rye and quinoa. Pearl barley has the husk partially or fully removed, so look for the higher fibre creamy brown grains rather than polished white.

Did you know?

Because in Britain we eat lots of potatoes, they make a great contribution to our vitamin C intake. New potatoes contain the most.

Fibre in breakfast cereals

Product	Average portion size	Fibre content g
All Bran	6 tbsp	10.3
Porridge, home made	1 bowl	1.3
Wheat biscuit cereal	2 biscuits	3.9
Shredded Wheat cereal	2 biscuits	4.4
Cornflakes	5 tbsp	0.3
Unsweetened muesli	3 tbsp	3.4

Apart from energy and fibre, whole grains are good sources of essential B group vitamins, zinc and iron.

This food group, too, is a great source of fibre, and apart from preventing constipation in pregnancy, fibre can help keep pregnancy blood sugars more even, and reduce the risk of other pregnancy complications including pre-eclampsia.

Although there is no additional requirement for fibre in pregnancy in the UK, achieving the minimum of 18g per day can be difficult. Eating whole grains or whole meal versions where possible can make a significant impact. The fibre content of some typical breakfast cereals are listed above.

Another measure of carbohydrate quality is the glycaemic index, and studies indicate that the risk of pregnancy diabetes increases if you eat high GI foods (see below).

Glycaemic index

This measures how a particular food affects your blood glucose when you eat it. The lower the GI, the better. A low GI means the carbohydrate is released slowly so that you stay feeling fuller for longer, and your body doesn't have a rush of blood sugar followed by a slump.

Studies have shown that mums to be who eat high GI foods, which are released more quickly, are more likely to have high sugar levels in pregnancy and pregnancy complications. If you have pregnancy diabetes, you should eat low GI foods as these help to keep your blood sugar under better control. The table below shows you how to choose lower GI foods.

GI of starchy carbohydrate foods

0-55 is low

56-69 is moderate

70 and over is high

Food	Glycaemic index
White bread	70
Whole meal bread	69
Stoneground whole meal bread	53
Rye bread	50
White boiled rice	98
White boiled basmati rice	58
Brown rice	68
Whole meal pasta e.g spaghetti	37
White pasta e.g spaghetti	41
Udon noodles	62
Pearl barley	25
Porridge with water	42
Potatoes, new boiled	62
Potatoes, boiled	56
Potatoes, mashed	70
Potatoes, baked	85
Couscous	65
Quinoa	53
Bulgur (cracked wheat)	46
All Bran	38
Cornflakes	93
Muesli	56
Wheat biscuit cereal	69
Rye crackers	64

Fruits

The choice is almost endless these days as new varieties appear frequently in our markets. Try to eat seasonally when you can, not forgetting old British favourites such as rhubarb, gooseberries, plums, apples and pears.

Fruit is a pregnancy essential as it provides a wide variety of different vitamins, minerals and protective plant nutrients (phytochemicals). A great source of vitamin C (for the maximum amount, eating ripe fruit raw and in season is about as good as it gets) and sometimes betacarotene, fruits also provide essential dietary fibre. One of the reasons that fruit juice only counts once in your five a day is that it contains almost no fibre, so make sure you have whole fruit as well as juice.

Many of the phytochemicals found in fruits (and other plant foods) act as antioxidants and prevent cells being damaged. There are many thousands of these and as some are only just being identified, researchers have not yet pinpointed those that may be of special benefit in pregnancy. However, the benefits of having plenty of whole fruits in the diet is well known.

- Red grapes and cranberries contain resveratrol, which is not only thought to slow the ageing process, but it has anti-inflammatory properties which is great at any stage of life.
- Apples and berries contain quercetin, another protective antioxidant
- Strawberries are not only a rich source of vitamin C, but also provide folate, and a protective antioxidant, ellagic acid.
- Papaya contains large quantities of both vitamin C and betacarotene.
- Many fruits contain potassium, which is important in regulating blood pressure, and the much-derided prune is an excellent source.
- Melon, especially cantaloupe is packed with betacarotene.
- Bioflavonoids of which grapefruit are a particularly rich source may help reduce water retention and swelling in the legs, a common pregnancy problem.
- Red and purple berries contain antioxidants called anthocynanins which are thought to help reduce the risk of developing cancers and heart disease by protecting cells from damage.

Nutritional benefits of different fruits

Item	Average portion	Approx Kcal	Why it's a great pregnancy snack
Apple	1 medium	46	Few calories, filling, thirst quenching, cheap, provides fibre, low GI
Apricots (ready to eat)	3 medium	75	Rich source of fibre; source of iron, and betacarotene. Easy to store
Bananas	1 medium	95	Easy to eat and digest, provides fibre and potassium, medium GI
Blueberries	2 handfuls	50	Great antioxidant protection
Kiwi fruit	2 fruit	40	Rich source of vitamin C, and potassium
Oranges	1 medium	45	Rich source vitamin C. Source of folate and low GI
Peaches	1 medium	36	Source of vitamin C, thirst quenching, cheap in season
Pears	1 medium	51	Source of fibre, cheap in season
Pineapple	1 large slice	33	Source of vitamin C, thirst quenching,
Plums	2 medium	28	Cheap in season, source betacarotene and fibre
Prunes (ready to eat)	3 medium	56	Rich in fibre, potassium, contains iron. Easy to store
Strawberries	7 strawberries	27	Rich source of vitamin C, and antioxidants. Best when in season

Vegetables

These also come in different colours — green, purple, white, orange and red — and the differently coloured ones contain a variety of vitamins, minerals and phytochemicals, which are essential for you and your growing baby. Eating five portions of vegetables a day as well as a fruit or glass of fruit juice will ensure you have a daily supply of baby building essentials.

Carrots and other orange coloured vegetables such as sweet potatoes and squash supply carotenoids, a form of betacarotene and vitamin A. Surprisingly, so do dark green veggies such as kale and spinach. Not only does vitamin A protect you by boosting immunity, it is essential for your baby's development especially that of her lungs.

Many vegetables are rich in folate, too. Asparagus, beetroot, purple sprouting broccoli, endive, spinach leaves, Swiss chard, baby sweet corn, Brussels sprouts all contain more than 80 mcg of folate per 80 g portion. If cooking, steam them lightly to preserve as much of this heat sensitive vitamin as possible.

Green leafy vegetables are a great source of magnesium, which you and your baby need. Magnesium is at the heart of the green plant pigment chlorophyll, so if it's green you'll be getting some! Seaweed is a good source of iodine. However brown

All the colours of the rainbow
Fruits come in different colours and each signals different nutrients and phytochemicals. Make sure you eat from across the range.

Red *strawberries, red grapes, red apples, raspberries, rhubarb, plums, redcurrants, red grapefruit.*

Green *kiwi fruit, green grapes, green apples, gooseberries, avocado.*

Yellow *pears, pineapples, some melons.*

Purple *blueberries, plums, cherries, blackcurrants, blackberries.*

Orange *clementines and satsumas, apricots, melons, sharon fruit, mango, papaya, nectarines and peaches.*

vegetables

Did you know?
Some vegetables provide iron, but it is less well absorbed by the body than the iron found in meat or other animal foods. However, to make sure you absorb as much as possible, avoid drinking tea or coffee at meal times, and have a vitamin C rich food at the same meal. A glass of unsweetened citrus juice, a few cherry tomatoes, a kiwi fruit or bowl of seasonal strawberries are all great candidates.

seaweeds (kelp, kombu, wakame, quandai-cai, hiziki/hijiki, arame or Sargassum fusiforme) which are usually sold for stews, contain so much you could overdose on the iodine, which could adversely effect your baby's health. Choose the lower iodine containing red or green seaweeds which are sold for sushi (e.g Nori) instead.

Herbs

Although the green part of plants used to flavour or season a dish are unlikely to have any medicinal benefit (due to the small amount normally used), herbs can add small quantities of vitamins, minerals and phytochemicals. Parsley is a great source of vitamin C for example, but you would have to munch through a 45 g bunch to have the same amount as eating one orange. Wash any herbs before use, making sure they do not have any soil left on them.

Milk, cheese and yogurt

Known for their contribution to calcium intakes, milk, yogurt and cheese have other baby building credentials, such as protein, iodine, vitamin B_2 (riboflavin) and B_{12} (cyanocobalamin). If you don't or can't eat this food group, it is really important to ensure that you are getting equivalent nutrition from alternative foods (see box, page 23). Substituting soya products for milk and yogurt is great, but make sure that they are fortified, especially if you don't eat meat as well (see also page 24).

Aim to have at least three portions of dairy products or equivalent a day. Your 700 mg calcium requirement can be met by:

TAKE CARE

Some unpasteurised, mould ripened or blue varieties of cheese carry a risk of listeriosis, which can have serios pregnancy complications (see also page 31).

Calcium-rich recipes
- *Stuffed Portobello Mushrooms*
- *Sardine and Red Pepper Strudel*
- *Egg, Tomato and Onion Roll*
- *Cheddar and Sundried Tomato Scones*

- 250 ml glass semi-skimmed milk + 130 g pot low fat yogurt + 30 g piece hard cheese *or*
- 250 g glass fortified soya 'milk' + 1 large canned sardine with bones *or*
- 100 g tofu + 1 tbsp sesame seeds + 2 ready-to-eat figs.

Meat and poultry

Although these foods are known for their high protein content they are packed with other important vitamins and minerals, which your body absorbs easily, especially during pregnancy.

Meats and poultry are, in general, great sources of iron, zinc and vitamin B_{12} but some provide a particularly rich source of certain nutrients. For example, pork for thiamin (B_1), beef for iron, turkey for zinc and niacin and lamb and beef for vitamin B_{12}. However, liver and any liver products such as paté or paste, should be avoided because they can have unhealthily high levels of retinol (vitamin A).

Pro- and prebiotics in pregnancy

Probiotic (cultures containing 'good' bacteria) mini yogurt based drinks are frequently consumed and are safe in pregnancy — just ensure you stick to use-by dates. A few studies have looked at whether probiotics may actually improve the health of pregnant women and one found that women who took probiotic supplements were less likely to suffer from pregnancy diabetes. However, further studies need to be carried out to confirm this as well as discover if prebiotics (substances often naturally found in certain items such as leeks and bananas, on which 'good' gut bacteria may grow) have other benefits to mother and her growing baby.

Did you know?

Duck contains more healthy monounsaturated fat than saturated fat. By grilling or dry frying a duck breast and removing the skin, you will consume less than 200 kcal yet receive around half of your pregnancy needs for zinc, and more than a third for iron. If you include the skin, the amount of fat obviously increases but so does the flavour! Perhaps an occasional treat?

Calcium rich alternatives

Calcium is an essential mineral in pregnancy and when nursing so ensure you have some of these calcium rich alternatives if you don't have milk, yogurt or cheese regularly.

- *Tofu*
- *Sardines or other canned fish with bones*
- *Fortified soya milk or yogurt*
- *Baked beans*
- *Curly kale or spinach*
- *Figs, especially dried or ready to eat*

Meat has had a lot of negative press over the last few years with concerns about its link to cancer, and its saturates content. Whilst there are issues with consuming lots of processed meats such as sausages, salamis and poor quality burgers, eating lean red meat with all visible fat removed a couple of times a week does not pose a danger. Indeed, the zinc, iron and vitamin B_{12}, which are provided and readily absorbed from meat supply dietary essentials. Whether you are planning a pregnancy or already pregnant, unless for religious or ethical reasons you can't or don't eat meat, do try to include lean meat in your diet at least once a week.

Fish and shellfish

Another great source of protein, fish also provide iodine and, to a lesser or greater degree depending on the variety, the very long chain fatty acids known as omega 3. Some fish are also rich in vitamins A and D. However, some fish contain unacceptable levels of mercury and/or other chemicals (see page 32).

Fish are grouped into two major types — white and oily. White fish such as haddock, cod, coley, pollack, red mullet, tilapia, plaice, sole, flounder, dab, etc., are safe to eat in pregnancy and are very low in fat but contain very little omega 3.

Oily fish such as trout, salmon, herring, mackerel, sardines, pilchards, anchovies and sprats are safe to eat in pregnancy and are a great source of omega 3 fatty acids and provide essential vitamins A and D.

Shellfish such as mussels, prawns, crab, lobster, langoustine, crayfish and squid are safe to eat in pregnancy when cooked. They all contain, iodine, selenium and copper and mussels, squid and crab contain omega 3. Avoid oysters as these are usually eaten raw.

Eggs, pulses and soya

These foods are great for non-meat eaters, supplying a range of different types of nutrients. Each has its own benefits, so try to eat a little of them all.

When choosing eggs, look for the British Lion mark stamp, which means the eggs have come from flocks vaccinated against Salmonella enteritidis, a common cause of food poisoning. Cook them thoroughly to reduce the risk of food poisoning bacteria.

Pulses are beans, peas and lentils and are a cheap supply of protein as well as B group vitamins, iron and zinc. Black eye beans are unusually high in folate: three tablespoons provide 60 per cent of your daily requirement. Lentils and most beans provide at least 2 mg of iron per 100 g portion.

Soya beans are an amazingly versatile food and the only bean, which contains all eight essential amino acids making it of equal to the protein of animal foods. The boiled beans are a good source of iron,

---

Easy ways with fish

- *Mash one canned sardine with lemon juice and spread on wholemeal toast, grill until hot.*
- *Microwave a skinless salmon fillet and whilst it is cooking stir fry two chopped spring onions, slices of red pepper and mangetout and a handful of beansprouts. Stir in a sauce made with 1tsp grated ginter, garlic, splash of sherry and 1 tsp reduced salt soy sauce. Serve with wholewheat or udon noodles.*
- *Place a white fish fillet on a few fine asparagus spears, top with chopped marinated artichokes, grated lemon zest, a squirt of lemon juice and bake for 20 minutes.*
- *Heat one tablespoon of rapeseed oil in a pan and quickly fry a large handful of raw prawns and a clove of crushed garlic until prawns are pink. Serve on top of a bed of leaves with a granary roll for a quick lunch.*

Nutritional content of eggs

Nutrient	Amount in one egg	% of Pregnancy requirement
Vitamin A mcg	98	16
Vitamin D mcg	0.9	9
Vitamin B2	0.24	22
Vitamin B12 mcg	1.3	86
Iodine mcg	27	19
Selenium mcg	6	10

folate, biotin and provide dietary fibre. Tofu or bean curd is a rich source of calcium, and also contains some iron.

If you are a vegan, beware having too many soya products as soya contains factors that can interfere with your body's ability to absorb and use iodine.

Nuts and seeds

These are a great source of vitamin E, the shorter omega 3 fatty acids, which the body can convert to long chain omega 3 fatty acids. Some are a great source of individual nutrients, but normally you only eat only small amounts. The following are 'super rich' in various nutrients:

- Sesame seeds in calcium, iron, magnesium and copper.
- Pumpkin seeds in iron, magnesium, and zinc.
- Sunflower seeds in magnesium, and vitamin E.
- Linseed (flax) in zinc and magnesium.
- Brazil nuts in selenium and vitamin E.
- Almonds in biotin (they also contain calcium).
- Hazelnuts in biotin and vitamin E.
- Peanuts in vitamin E and biotin.

Seeds are a key supply of magnesium, an important pregnancy mineral, so nibbling them can boost your supply.

Water and other drinks

Being hydrated in pregnancy is crucial and even more so when you are breastfeeding. I even devoted an entire book, *Super Drinks for Pregnancy*, to the subject. It contains dozens of recipes accompanied by full nutritional analyses.

Mums to be should drink around 2.3 litres (4 pints) of fluids a day and breastfeeding mums around 2.6–2.7 litres (4¾ pts). It is expected that 70–80 per cent of this fluid will come from drinks including water, and the remainder from water-containing foods (especially vegetables and fruit).

Fluids can be water or watery drinks such as herbal and fruit teas, milk or milky drinks and fruit juices or smoothies. However you will want to limit your intake of caffeine containing drinks such as green and black teas and coffee as more than 200 mg caffeine per day is not recommended (see page 35).

Carbonated flavoured drinks, even diet versions, provide few nutrients, and it would be better to drink a glass of milk or water — both for your teeth and

the nutrition your baby receives. It is also very easy to over-consume calories by drinking sweetened drinks and drinking large amounts could increase your risk of having pregnancy diabetes. So limit the number of sugary drinks you have. One glass of fruit juice or a smoothie a day is sufficient.

Fatty, sugary and oily foods

No one could argue that cakes, biscuits, ice cream or chocolates are pregnancy essentials even though cravings can make them seem so. They add very little to your diet and may displace healthier foods, so limit the amount you eat. If you do eat them, choose small portions, and have some milk and/or a piece of fruit first. This way you will obtain vital nutrients and have less space for the less nutritious treat.

Oils and dressings are usually high in fat, so limit these, using oils high in monounsaturated fatty acids such as olive or rapeseed oil. Try balsamic glaze or a spritz of lemon juice on your salad, or choose the lowest fat mayonnaise or mix some with fat-free yogurt. Butter is high in saturates so either replace with a mono- or polyunsaturated spread, preferably reduced in fat, or use a reduced fat butter if you can't give up the taste.

All sugars, syrups and honey are similar in their energy value. Try to have as little as possible, being even more strict if you have pregnancy diabetes. Use one of the many sugar substitutes now available; all are safe in pregnancy. Xylitol is included in some of the recipes.

Salty foods

Most condiments are fine to eat in pregnancy but be careful with salt. Most people far exceed the daily 6g recommendation. Take care not to have too many savoury snacks, salted nuts, pickles, olives, sausages,

Did you know?
Mycoprotein such as Quorn is a rich source of zinc, and fibre, too, and comes in a variety of easy forms for cooking.

bacon, salami and other preserved meats. Many everyday foods, which also are high in salt include breads, cheeses and many ready meals and soups.

Key supplements

Apart from the 400 mcg of folic acid you need from before you conceive until the 12th week of pregnancy, make sure you also take a supplement which contains 10 mcg of vitamin D. These two vitamins in supplement form are pregnancy essentials which are not easily obtained in the required amounts from foods.

If you want to take an all round supplement look out for pregnancy supplements which have been formulated to take into account your increased nutrient requirements using safe levels of vitamins and minerals. Some also supply essential omega 3 fatty acids. Do not use cod liver oil or other fish oil supplements if they contain vitamin A as retinol.

Strict vegetarians are advised to carefully plan their diet, and an comprehensive multivitamin and mineral supplement is recommended.

Best for folate
An 80 g portion of the following contains more than 80 mcg of folate. Steam lightly to preserve as much of this heat sensitive vitamin as possible.

- Asparagus, steamed
- Beetroot, boiled or roasted
- Purple sprouting broccoli
- Endive, raw
- Spinach leaves, raw
- Swiss chard, boiled
- Baby sweetcorn, boiled
- Brussel sprouts boiled

key supplements

CHAPTER 3

LOOKING AFTER YOURSELF

Food supplies you with the vital nutrients necessary to maintain a pregnancy and support your baby's growth so it's important to know which ones to avoid and how to prepare food safely. Managing your weight also has a great impact on the health of you and your baby.

WEIGHT CONCERNS

Being the 'right' weight when you conceive gives your baby a great start in life, but many pregnancies are unplanned, so you may need to make adjustments. Being pregnant does not give you a green light to eat for two. The more unnecessary weight you gain, the harder it is to shift afterwards, and your baby needs a healthy active mum at all times. If you are over-weight at the start of your pregnancy, it's really important to manage your weight. The greater your weight, especially with a BMI >30, the greater the risk of:

- Having a baby with birth defects (e.g. spina bifida or cleft lip or palate);
- Miscarriage or still birth;
- Pre eclampsia;
- Pregnancy diabetes;
- Complications in labour, including having a Caesarean section.

Being very overweight can also increase your baby's risk of long-term health problems. It is now believed that what happens to your baby whilst you are carrying her can influence the way she responds to a host of factors after birth and into later life. Looking after yourself in pregnancy and eating a healthy diet, along with avoiding gaining too much weight is important to minimise the effect of this 'metabolic programming'.

Overly thin mums to be tend to have underweight babies and are more at risk of miscarriage. Women who have a BMI of 18.5 or less often find it difficult to conceive, and may be advised to gain some weight before trying to get pregnant. If you are underweight because you restrict your diet in any way — whether you have an eating disorder, eschew certain food groups, or are particularly choosy — it is really important to deal with these issues before you become pregnant. Your baby needs a constant supply of nutrients and relies on you eating a healthy balanced diet to provide a wide range of vitamins, minerals and crucially the energy from carbohydrates, fat and protein. Dieting and bingeing are off limits in pregnancy.

How much weight should I gain?

You obviously need to make sure you are eating enough, but how much is that really when, after your baby is born, you don't want to have to worry about months of hard work to get your figure back.

Guidance on how much you should gain is less clear in the UK than in other countries. After the booking appointment, most women are not regularly weighed unless they started pregnancy very overweight (BMI >30). In some other countries, regular weighing is part of antenatal check ups. Currently there are no prescriptive guidelines as to how much weight gain is acceptable in pregnancy. However, the USA Institute of Medicine guidelines (2009) provide a useful guide for weight gain based on your pre pregnancy weight (see overleaf).

Measuring weight

Although it has some limitations, most health professionals use body mass index to assess weight. BMI is measured by dividing your weight in kilograms by your height in metres squared. So if you weigh 70 kg (11 stone) and you are 1.68 m (5 ft 6 in), your BMI is calculated as $70/1.68^2$. This is a BMI of 24.8 just in the normal healthy weight range.

Weight gain for singleton pregnancy

Pre-pregnancy weight status	BMI	Recommended gain kg / lbs
Underweight	<18.5	12.5–18 / 28–40
Healthy weight	18.5–24.9	11.5–16 / 25–35
Overweight	25.0–29.9	7.0–11.5 / 15–25
Obese	>30.0	5.0–9.0 / 11–20

Weight gain for twin+ pregnancy

Pre-pregnancy weight status	BMI	Recommended gain kg / lbs
Normal	18.5–24.9	17–25 / 37–54
Overweight	25–29.9	14–23 / 31–50
Obese	>30	11–19 / 25–42

Your energy needs

Like most mums, you may be somewhat surprised to discover that you really don't need to eat more for the first two trimesters. Your body is amazing at utilising what you eat as well as your body stores to supply your baby with many of her needs. Throughout pregnancy, different hormones are used to mobilise your stores of fat and nutrients and your digestive system becomes increasing efficient at absorbing nutrients from foods. This, coupled with a decrease in

Where does the weight go?

You can expect to gain an average of 12.5 kg (30 lbs) throughout your pregnancy and here is where the weight goes.

Breast and uterus enlargement	*1.3 kg (3 lbs)*
Placenta	*0.7 kg (2 lbs)*
Baby	*3–3.5 kg (7–8 lbs)*
Amniotic fluid	*0.7 kg (2 lbs)*
Additional blood and fluids	*3 kg (7 lbs)*
Fat deposits for breastfeeding	*3.5 kg (8 lbs)*

Stay active

Being physically active is a great way to help manage your weight even when pregnant; it also can help your body prepare for labour, increase your stamina and keep you supple. Most women are able to carry out some exercise whether it is simply walking, doing housework or gardening, or carrying on with a routine at the gym or swimming pool. Activity of any sort also can help control your blood sugar levels which may reduce your risk of developing pregnancy diabetes.

Your body adapts to exercise during pregnancy and this seems to protect your baby from potential harm so not only is doing some gentle exercise good for you and your baby now, it can help you return to your pre pregnancy weight sooner. You are also:

- *less likely to develop high blood pressure and pre-eclampsia;*
- *have better mental health during your pregnancy because of the feel-good hormones you produce when activ*
- *less likely to have back problems or varicose veins.*

activity levels as pregnancy continues, means that most women only need to increase the amount of calories they consume in the last trimester, and this is only a modest 200 kcal.

However, if you started pregnancy underweight you may be advised to eat more than usual for the first three months as this is a critical time for fetal development. But if you started pregnancy overweight (BMI 26-30) you should eat healthily and keep active, aiming to keep your weight gain to a minimum until the last trimester.

Later on, if you breastfeed, you will find it very energy intensive and recent UK recommendations are for an extra 335 kcal per day for the first six months.

Expecting twins or more

Although there are no specific guidelines in the UK for nutrition for twin or multiple pregnancies, it is generally accepted that there is a need for additional calories and nutrients. In fact, gaining adequate weight in the first 20 weeks predicts a higher birth weight for the babies. See chart on the opposite page for the US Institute of Medicine recommendations on how much to gain for single and twin pregnancies.

MAKING SAFE FOOD CHOICES

It seems that almost every week there's something new about what we can or can't eat — pregnant or not. While this can be very worrying, with a little common sense and some food knowledge, it is simple to avoid what may be risky without denying yourself enjoyable and nutritious foods.

Food safety is important at any stage of life, but while pregnant, extra care is needed as you and your baby are more vulnerable to illness. By being vigilant about food storage and hygiene, and avoiding just a few foods, you can keep hazards away.

Cheese

Many cheeses are safe to eat in pregnancy and are a great source of protein, calcium and phosphorus. The risk from some cheeses is listeriosis, which is a flu-like illness that can cause miscarriage or stillbirth.

Cheeses that are safe to eat include:

- All hard cheeses such as Cheddar, Cheshire, Leicestershire, Gouda, Edam, Gruyère, etc.;
- Hard, unpasteurised varieties such as Parmesan or Pecorino;
- Soft cheeses such as feta, halloumi, cottage, cream, mascarpone, mozzarella.

However, make sure you avoid:

- Unpasteurised, soft sheep, cow or goat's cheeses;

High protein diets

It matters in pregnancy where your energy comes from. A healthy pregnancy diet provides a good balance of carbohydrates, fats and proteins. Eating a high-protein diet means that you are likely to have too few carbohydrates and possibly too much fat. The consequences for your baby are still being investigated but there is some evidence that very high intakes of protein could influence a baby's long-term health.

- Mould-ripened cheeses such as brie, Camembert and chevre (a goat's cheese);
- Blue-veined cheeses such as Stilton, blue Shropshire, gorgonzola, Danish blue, etc., unless you cook them thoroughly, which will kill any listeria bacteria which could be present.

Fish and shellfish
These highly nutritious foods are good sources of protein, omega 3 fatty acids and iodine. They should be part of your pregnancy diet but bear in mind:
- All white fish, such as cod, haddock, coley, saithe, sole and whiting is safe to eat.
- Oily fish, such as mackerel, salmon, herring, sardines, pilchards and trout can be eaten up to twice a week in pregnancy.
- Tuna is safe to eat but in limited amounts as it accumulates some mercury as it ages and grows. Smaller species such as skipjack or yellowfin are likely to contain less mercury and other pollutants than albacore or 'white' tuna. In the UK, the recommended amount, which some say is unnecessarily conservative, is to have only two 140 g portions of fresh tuna a week, or four 140 g portions of canned tuna.
- Some large fish — marlin, king-mackerel, tilefish, swordfish and shark — should not be eaten because they can contain methyl mercury.
- Raw fish is not safe to eat as it may contain tiny worms, which are destroyed when frozen or cooked. Freshly made raw fish sushi is not safe to eat. However, most sushi available in super-markets or restaurants has, by law, to have been made using frozen fish. If you are in any doubt, ask if the fish has been frozen. If yes, then it is safe to eat. In the UK, it is considered safe to eat smoked salmon; the risk of food-borne infection is very low.

Nuts and seeds
Peanuts and other nuts, seeds such as sesame, or foods containing them such as peanut butter or tahini, are safe to eat during your pregnancy unless you have an allergy to them or your health professional suggests you avoid them.

Eggs and foods made with raw eggs
You can eat any style eggs provided the white and yolk are fully cooked. Home-made mayonnaise, sorbets and some desserts such as tiramisu, cold soufflés or mousses made with raw eggs could contain salmonella so are not safe to eat. Shop-bought versions of these are safe to eat. If you are eating out and are unsure whether your meal contains raw egg, make sure to ask.

Seaweed
If eaten dried or used in breads, seaweed is safe as are red and brown ones often used for sushi. Sushi must be made from frozen fish to be safe to eat.

> ## Polychlorinated biphenyls (PCBs)
> *You may have heard that some foods, including fish, may contain 'persistent organic pollutants' and dioxins. These chemicals are unlikely to pose a major risk to you or your baby, as their level is extremely low and the benefits of eating fish far outweigh the risk of their presence. So don't stop eating fish because of this slim possibility.*

TAKE CARE

Shellfish such as mussels, prawns and crab is all fine to eat in pregnancy provided it has been cooked properly so that any bacteria or viruses it may be contaminated with are killed. Raw shellfish such as oysters or other uncooked shellfish should not be eaten.

SAFE FOOD PREPARATION TECHNIQUES

By following basic food hygiene you can avoid food - borne illnesses that can harm you and your baby.

- *Always wash your hands with soap and water before handling food and especially after you have been to the toilet, handled rubbish, touched pets or changed nappies.*
- *Also wash your hands after handling raw meat, fish or poultry.*
- *Wear gloves when gardening and if you have a pet, wear gloves to move any animal waste or to change the litter box (better still, have someone else do so). Toxoplasmosis parasites live in animal faeces and can cause blindness and brain damage in babies.*
- *Keep your kitchen and food serving area really clean. Bleach cloths and work surfaces regularly; wash tea towels daily and don't use as hand towels.*
- *As soon as possible after shopping, transfer your food to the fridge; do not leave it in a warm place such as the office or car.*
- *Store foods at the right temperature, checking that your fridge is below 5°C (40°F). The most perishable foods such as cooked meats, soft cheeses, salad leaves, ready meals and desserts need to be kept the coolest.*
- *Use the salad bin at the bottom of your fridge for unwashed fruits and vegetables.*
- *Wrap or place in containers any raw meat or fish which may drip onto other foods and place in the coldest part of the fridge.*

- *Keep eggs in the fridge.*
- *Check use by and best before dates on foods and stick to them. Throw out foods which are date expired and don't be tempted to buy reduced short life products at the supermarket.*
- *When preparing foods keep one board for raw meat and fish and another for cooked foods to prevent cross contamination.*
- *Make sure you wash all fresh fruit before you eat it to reduce the risk of microbial infection, and to remove any dirt or fungicidal sprays. If a fruit has become rotten or mouldy, even in one small part, throw it away.*
- *Make sure that when you cook meat it is cooked through. It needs to reach at least 70°C (160°F) internally, which you can check with a meat probe. Another indication is when the juices run clear when you insert a sharp knife to the centre of the meat.*

Brown seaweeds such as kelp and some of the imported Japanese seaweeds, however, are very high in iodine, so they should not be eaten.

Liver, liver products and pâtés
Due to their very high levels of vitamin A, which could cause damage to a developing baby, women who are pregnant or planning to become pregnant are advised to avoid all forms of liver and liver products (terrines, pâtés, pastes, etc.)
Pâtés that you buy from the delicatessen counter may also be made from other meats, fish or vegetables,

which also are prone to listeria contamination. If pâtés have been heat treated by canning, or you make your own being strict with food hygiene, they should be safe.

Ready-to-eat meals
Foods that have been partly or full prepared for you to reheat at home must be cooked through until piping hot to kill any harmful bacteria.

Alcohol

This topic so regularly hits the headlines it is difficult to keep up with the latest advice on whether or not you should avoid alcohol altogether or you can have the odd glass now and then. In 2007, the UK Department of Health made it clear that pregnant women should not drink alcohol, but if they choose to do so, they should not drink more than one or two units once or twice a week. However, other experts say that there is no safe limit.

Many women fall pregnant unexpectedly and it may take them a little while to realise that they are pregnant. Perhaps if you are one of these women, you may be anxious because had you known you were pregnant, you wouldn't have drunk alcohol. If this is the case, the best advice is to stop drinking alcohol as soon as you know that you are pregnant, and talk to your healthcare provider if you have any concerns.

The effect of alcohol on your baby

Alcohol from your bloodstream passes from through the placenta to your baby, where his liver breaks it down. However, your baby's liver is not mature enough to do this effectively until you are at least half way through your pregnancy.

It is clear from many studies that heavy drinkers are more likely to have babies who suffer from Fetal Alcohol Spectrum Disorder (FASD) whose symptoms include low birth weight and facial deformities as well as learning difficulties and psychiatric problems.

Babies born to binge drinkers (those having more than 7.5 units of alcohol on a single occasion) tend to be born prematurely and of low birth weight; there is a higher incidence of miscarriage and still birth than for women who don't drink alcohol.

Caffeinated drinks

Going off coffee can be one of the early signs that you are pregnant, but even if you can still tolerate it, how much should you be drinking whilst you are expecting or should you give it up altogether? In 2008, the UK government advised women that if they were planning a pregnancy or were pregnant that they should keep their caffeine intake to no more

What is a unit of alcohol?

Drink and strength (Alcohol by volume ABV)	Amount	Units of alcohol
White wine 13%	Standard glass 175 ml	2.3
White wine 13%	Large glass 250 ml	3.3
White wine 11%	Standard glass 175 ml	1.9
White wine 11%	Large glass 250 ml	2.8
Champagne 12%	Standard glass 175 ml	2.1
Champagne 12%	Large glass 250 ml	3.0
Red wine 14%	Standard glass 175 ml	2.5
Red wine 14%	Large glass 250 ml	3.5
Red wine 12%	Standard glass 175 ml	2.1
Red wine 12%	Large glass 250 ml	3.0
Rose wine 10%	Standard glass 175 ml	1.8
Rose wine 10%	Large glass 250 ml	2.5
Spirit (gin/ vodka) 37.5%	Single shot 25 ml	0.9
Spirit (gin/ vodka) 37.5%	Large single shot 35 ml	1.3
Spirit (gin/vodka) 37.5%	Double shot 50 ml	1.9
Alcopop 4%	700 ml (70 cl) bottle	2.8
Alcopop 4%	275 ml bottle	1.1
Alcopop 5%	700 ml (70 cl) bottle	3.5
Alcopop 5%	275 ml bottle	1.4
Cider 4.5%	440 ml can	2.0
Cider 7.5%	275 ml bottle	2.1
Cider 7.5%	500 ml can	3.8
Lager 4%	330 ml bottle	1.3
Lager 4%	440 ml can	1.8
Lager 5%	440 ml can	2.2

than 200 mg (that's about two small coffees). Large intakes of caffeine have been linked to infertility, low birth weight babies and miscarriage.

When considering your caffeine intake, it's important to bear in mind that caffeine is not only found in coffee, tea and cola but also in energy drinks, chocolate and cocoa as well as in many cold and flu remedies.

With chocolate, the darker the chocolate, the higher the amount of caffeine, though in real terms this is not significant unless you are eating several bars of chocolate each day!

Energy drinks, which contain more than 150mg of caffeine per litre, must declare their caffeine content according to an EU code of practice. They should carry a statement warning that they are 'not suitable for children, pregnant women and persons sensitive to caffeine'. As you can see from the table below, an energy drink often contains less caffeine than a cup of coffee, but it is important that you are aware of the amount in a range of beverages.

As you'll know from the coffee shops you visit, the strength of the brew may be determined by the barista. In the UK, the Food Standards Agency Food Surveillance Unit has measured caffeine levels in beverages, both brewed domestically as well as in the laboratory. Not surprisingly there are differences and these are shown by the range of measurements in the table opposite.

Decaffeinated coffees and teas are great alternatives in pregnancy and you may also like herb or fruit teas. They can be refreshing and some have benefits of their own. Camomile is said to enhance sleep and peppermint aids digestion. Raspberry leaf tea is reputed to ease labour and strengthen the uterus when taken in the last trimester, but don't drink it before then as it has been linked to miscarriage.

My book, *Superdrinks for Pregnancy,* provides lots of delicious and healthy alternatives to caffeinated and alcoholic drinks.

Comparison of caffeine-containing items

Item	Quantity (approx)	Estimated amount of caffeine/Source
Instant coffee	One mug (260 ml)	100*
	One cup (190 ml)	75*
Black tea, infusion	One mug (260 ml)	50-75*
	One cup (190 ml)	33-50*
Drinking chocolate	Made as per pack instructions (200 ml)	1.1-8.2*
Filter coffee	Small (225 ml)	160+
	Medium (350 ml)	240+
	Large (450 ml)	320+
Cappuccino or latte	Small (225 ml)	75+
	Medium (350 ml)	75+
	Large (450 ml)	150+
Mocha	Small (225 ml)	90+
	Medium (350 ml)	95+
	Large (450 ml)	175+
Flat white	Small (225 ml)	150+
Americano coffee	Small (225 ml)	75+
	Medium (350 ml)	150+
	Large (450 ml)	225+
Energy drink (Red Bull)	473 ml can	151^
Cola drinks	330 ml can	11-70*
70% dark chocolate	40 g	6@
Milk chocolate	40 g	3@
Cocoa powder	As made 190 ml cup	<1@

* FSA Survey of Caffeine Levels in Hot Beverages, Food Information Sheet 53/04 April 2004, and FSA 2008
+ Starbucks nutritional information accessed March 2011. @ Green and Black's Organic Chocolate accessed March 2011 ^ Calculated from label

FOOD AND COMMON PREGNANCY COMPLAINTS

Some lucky women do sail through pregnancy with no complications or hiccups and really are the picture of health. But for others, pregnancy involves a range of health issues. Some can be managed by making changes to what and how you eat. Many of the more minor conditions are thought to be caused by the huge hormonal upheaval that characterises early pregnancy. Indeed, an aversion to certain foods can be one of the first signs of pregnancy.

Cravings and aversions

It is estimated that more than half of all pregnant women are affected by these, and the reasons why are not fully understood. One theory, which makes logical sense, is that if you suffer from nausea and vomiting while eating or drinking, it could be because your body is protecting your baby from potential harmful toxins. Aversions to coffee, meat, eggs, spicy foods and some vegetables are not uncommon, and generally shouldn't put you at a nutritional disadvantage if you find alternative nutrient-rich foods. So, for example, if you can't eat meat, try fish or other zinc- and iron-rich foods. If you can't drink coffee, try herbal tisanes instead.

Cravings, on the other hand, were once thought to be a sign that your body had a nutritional need. While this might be the true for commonly craved foods such as broccoli, milk or grapefruit, it does not explain some women's craving for non-foods, such as coal, ice or soil. Neither is there a nutritional need in craving low-nutrient foods, such as chocolate, cakes and biscuits! If you do want these sorts of foods, but are otherwise following a healthy diet, then go ahead and have a small portion. Just be sure that they don't fill you up and replace more nutritious foods.

Sickness and nausea

Both are early indicators of pregnancy and are not necessarily limited to the morning. The peak of sickness and nausea is usually around six to 18 weeks when your baby is particularly vulnerable, so they may be your body's ways of preventing you consuming foods, which could cause damage or promote miscarriage. A comprehensive review of various methods used to alleviate nausea done in

looking after yourself

2010 found that using ginger or vitamin B_6 were most effective.

- Have a slice of root ginger in hot water as your first drink of the day.
- Use fresh or ground ginger in your cooking.
- Sip on a low alcohol ginger beer or ale if you can tolerate the bubbles.
- Have a ginger supplement — up to 1 g is safe.
- Have a vitamin B_6 supplement — up to 50 mg is safe.

Heartburn

You may find that as you pregnancy progresses you suffer from a burning sensation in your throat as acid from your stomach is forced up the oesophagus. As with many pregnancy problems, it is caused by changes in your hormones, which relax the muscles controlling the valve at the entry to your stomach. As your baby grows, he also will 'squash' your internal organs. However there are some things to try:

- Avoid or limit chocolate, spicy or fatty foods, coffee, tea, carbonated or acidic drinks (fruit juice).
- Drink reduced fat milk to help 'settle' your stomach.
- Eat frequent small meals rather than a few large ones, and sit down for a while afterwards.
- Sleep more upright; prop yourself up with pillows.

Constipation

With this common pregnancy complaint, prevention is far preferable to 'cure', so make sure that you drink plenty of water and eat fibre-rich whole grain cereals and vegetables.

- Carry (and drink from!) a water bottle so you don't become dehydrated.
- Add lentils and beans to soups, stews and curries.
- Pop a packet of apricots, figs or prunes in your bag to nibble on.
- Use wholemeal bread, whole-grain cereals and opt for high-fibre muesli.
- Have baked beans on wholemeal toast or a jacket potato with skin for a quick high fibre lunch.
- Have peas and/or sweetcorn as regular vegetables.

Pregnancy diabetes

Also known as gestational diabetes, this is caused by your body failing to produce enough of the hormone insulin to control your blood glucose (sugar). Your need for insulin increases in pregnancy, and if you are not making enough, you will have too much glucose in your blood stream and this will pass through the placenta to your baby. This is dangerous for you and your baby and increases the risk that your baby will be large for her gestational age. You could also have other complications in pregnancy and labour unless the diabetes is properly managed. Adopting a healthy lifestyle throughout pregnancy will not only reduce your risk of developing the condition, but will also help you to manage it if you do develop it.

- Be particularly careful to eat whole-grain and minimally processed cereals, concentrating on low GI foods (see page 20).
- Avoid drinks that are high in sugars, whether natural or not, especially between meals.
- Plan your meals to include a source of protein, some vegetables and a low to medium GI carbohydrate food such as plain boiled potatoes, pearl barley or basmati rice.
- Avoid snacking on cakes, biscuits, ice cream or confectionery.

CHAPTER 4

MENU PLANS

A great deal of thought and hard work has gone into the creation of the recipes. My brief was to create healthy dishes — full of the nutrients that pregnant and new mums need — but also that taste great. But even with this array of dishes, it can be complicated to create varied meal plans that meet all your daily requirements. So to ensure you and your baby benefit from the right nutrients at the right times, I've devised special meal plans.

There are four different plans — one for each trimester and one for the newborn weeks. Each plan contains breakfasts, lunches, dinners, snacks and drinks, to ensure that your diet is varied, interesting and meets your specific requirements for the stage. Recipes from the book are italicised while the other suggestions can be store bought; all the selections ensure that your diet remains varied and interesting.

FIRST TRIMESTER

During the first few weeks of pregnancy, a lot is going on as your body adapts to your new state and your baby develops. All this development – your baby grows from a few microscopic cells to a being with all his or her major organs and systems – and the hormonal changes required to nourish the placenta can make you feeling exhausted, especially if you are quite nauseous or sick. By following my menu plan, you will keep well nourished, but if you can't stomach regular meals, the 'Little plates' provides a range of small nutritious meals and snacks.

Tiredness can also be due to anaemia, a lack of iron, or occasionally vitamin B_{12} or folic acid. If you didn't have a particularly good diet before pregnancy, are vegan, or don't eat much meat, especially red meat, then it may be worth having your iron stores checked. A simple blood test reveals this.

If you can't keep food down first thing, you may want to take some snacks or a simple breakfast with you to work.

- *Make or buy fruity smoothies (e.g. Berry Smoothie: made with 150 g mixed berries blended with 100 g plain yogurt; or see my book,* Superdrinks for Pregnancy, *for more ideas). An vaccum flask will keep them chilled on the train or bus.*
- *Pack a bag of dried fruit, nuts and seeds to nibble on, or some dried mango slices.*
- *Make a batch of Orange Bran Muffins, (page 151) and take one to work for a late breakfast along with a glass of milk.*
- *Sandwiches are great for breakfast too; avoid fatty mayonnaise rich fillings, opting for simple sliced meat or cheese with salads.*

If you are vomiting, it is important to replace the lost fluids, by drinking plenty. It doesn't matter if it is water, herbal tea, milk or diluted fruit juice. If you haven't gone off caffeine, regular tea or coffee is fine in limited amounts (see page 34). Some women find ginger helpful in alleviating nausea and may work for you. Ask your partner to bring you cup of hot water with a slice of fresh root ginger in bed in the morning, accompanied perhaps by a ginger snap or plain biscuit. Recipes which use ginger include: Teriyaki Turkey with Sesame Cucumber Salad (page 95) and Sea Bass with Pomegranate Salsa (page 114).

SECOND TRIMESTER

By now you may be starting to feel a little more energetic and may have regained your appetite as the nausea will probably have diminished. Although your calorie needs haven't yet increased, its important you follow my menu plan in order to eat the nutrient-rich foods that ensure your baby has sufficient vitamins and minerals for her development. Having extra energy, means its a good idea to cook some meals in

bulk and freeze them. When your baby arrives you will be very busy and tired and cooking is not likely to be a priority, so whether you or your partner do the cooking, get ahead with a bit of planning. You'll appreciate the few extra minutes that you spend chopping and cooking now when you are time-poor in the weeks after the birth.

If you haven't started to take vitamin D supplements, now is the time to do so, especially if you don't get out in the sun much, have dark skin or cover your skin for cultural reasons.

Try to eat more vitamin D-rich foods. Not many foods actually provide it but several of my recipes – Smoked Salmon Flakes with Herbed Lentils (page 116), Tuna Steaks with Sundried Tomato Crust and Lime Dressing (page 119), Mushroom and Asparagus Omelette (page 55), Sardine and Cheese Toastie (page 69) and Sprats with Avocado and Cherry Tomatoes (page 117) – provide at least one quarter of your day's needs.

Another great way of getting vitamin D is to enjoy a little sunshine — half an hour a day before 11 a.m. or after 3 p.m. will top up your stores without increasing your risk of cancer.

THIRD TRIMESTER

Your baby's brain and nervous system need the whole of your pregnancy to grow and mature, but in this trimester the process of myelination occurs, when a fatty sheath insulates nervous system. This requires the presence of vitamin B_{12} as well as an adequate supply (200 mg day) of the omega 3 fatty acid, DHA (docosahexaenoic acid). Ensuring you have some oily fish at least once but not more than twice a week will provide your baby with DHA . My menu plan and a variety of recipes in the book (see page 154) will ensure that it is the case.

If you don't eat fish, eat omega 3-fortified eggs or milk or linseed (flaxseed), sprinkled on cereals or salads or as a pressed oil used in salad dressings. Omega 6 fatty acids unfortunately compete with omega 3s for absorption in the body, so if you don't eat fish and rely on vegetarian sources for your omega 3 it's best not to have too much omega 6 in your diet. As sunflower spreads and oil are the commonest source of omega 6 in the diet, simply use

monounsaturate-rich oils and spreads such as rapeseed and olive instead of polyunsaturated sunflower, maize or peanut oils.

As your baby grows bigger, she will start to squash some of your internal organs and gut, and this can cause you to become constipated. To avoid this, drink plenty of fluids, at least 1.5–2 litres of water or other fluids each day, keep active, and top up on fibre-rich foods such as Raspberry Porridge with Walnuts (page 51), Orange Bran Muffins (page 151), Fruity Flapjack (page 149) and Herbed Barley (page 138). Eating normal size portions may again be difficult, so look at my 'Little Plates' recipes, which will give you the essential nutrients without filling you up too much.

BREASTFEEDING AND THE EARLY WEEKS WITH YOUR NEW BABY

Whether or not you are breastfeeding, you need to eat nourishing foods and rest when you can. If you are breastfeeding, you must ensure that your increased need for vitamins and minerals is met. My menu plan ensures this is the case.

Perhaps not surprisingly one of the greatest increases is in the amount of calcium you need. Try to have calcium rich snacks and milky drinks such as malted milk, cocoa or plain hot milk, when you sit down to feed your baby. Also prepare my recipes that use tofu, cheese, milk or yogurt, or contain canned fish with bones such as Berry Yogurt Breakfast (page 53), Bean and Salsa Wrap (page 68), Baba Ganoush (page 56), Roasted Baby Vegetables with Tofu (page 124), Crab Cakes with Watercress and Orange Salad (page 111) and Baked Figs with Pistachio and Honeyed Yogurt (page 146) as these all supply calcium, and many provide magnesium, zinc, copper and B vitamins, which are also needed in greater quantities.

Some babies who develop colic do seem to improve when their mother avoids certain foods. The culprits usually cited are garlic, onions, foods from the cabbage family, citrus fruits and even chocolate. So if you suspect your baby is unsettled when you eat one of these foods, omit it for a couple of days and see if there is an improvement. Chat to your health visitor if you are intending to make this sort of change to make sure you don't accidentally leave crucial nutrient-rich foods out of your diet.

menu plans

FIRST TRIMESTER

	Monday	Tuesday	Wednesday
breakfast	• *Raspberry Porridge with Walnuts* OR • Bran Flakes with sultanas OR • Scrambled egg on wholemeal toast with grilled tomatoes PLUS • Orange juice	• 2 boiled eggs with wholemeal roll and spread OR • Muesli with extra fruit OR • Greek yogurt with strawberries and honey PLUS • Berry smoothie (page 40)	• Muesli with yogurt and raspberries OR • 2 Weetabix with blueberries OR • Greek yogurt, fruit and seeds PLUS • Orange juice
lunch	• Greens soup OR • Carrot and coriander soup WITH • *Watercress and Salmon Salad* OR • *Egg, Tomato and Onion Roll* • Low fat fruit yogurt	• *Cos, Chicken and Croûton Salad* OR • *Ratatouille with Halloumi and Bread* OR • Baked beans on 2 slices wholemeal toast with spread • 2 clementines OR • 1 slice fresh pineapple	• *Smoked Mackerel, Ricotta and Beetroot Bruschetta* OR • *Pasta Primavera* OR • *Beef and Beet Sandwich* • *Carrot Tray Bake* OR • *Chocolate Brazil Brownie*
dinner	• *Sesame and Coriander Chicken with Mango Salsa* OR • *Greek Style Tomato and Haddock* OR • *Black Eye Bean, Currant and Fresh Mint Stew* WITH • *Almond Rice* OR • *Hot Potato Salad* AND • Steamed mangetout OR • Watercress and baby leaf salad with fat-free French dressing • *Baked Fig with Pistachios and Honey Yogurt* OR • *Strawberry Mousse*	• *Creamy Vegetarian Mince* WITH *Herbed Barley* OR • *Hungarian Goulash* WITH *Leek Mash* OR • *Chocolate and Chilli Chicken* WITH *Quinoa and Sunflower Seeds* WITH • *Green Chilli Edamame* OR • Steamed broccoli • *Mango and Lime Dessert* OR • *Summer Fruit Compote* (with xylitol) with 1 scoop vanilla ice cream	• *Turkey Herb Burger with Fruity Salsa* OR • *Vegetable Pancakes with Red Pepper Sauce* OR • *Sausage and Orzo Hotpot* WITH • Steamed broccoli • 2 plums OR • 1 pear
snacks	• 40 g ready-to-eat apricots • *Carrot Tray Bake*	• *Fruity Flapjack* • 1 chocolate digestive OR • 25 g chocolate-covered Brazil nuts	• Apple OR orange

DRINKS: 300 ml semi-skimmed milk or fortified soya equivalent in drinks throughout the day. Water ad lib throughout the day, and herb tea, coffee and tea as guided by chapter 3. Fruit juice assumed to be 200 ml glass unsweetened.

Thursday	Friday	Saturday	Sunday
• *Mushroom and Asparagus Omelette* OR • *Raisin and Apple Pancakes* OR • Currant bun and banana PLUS • *Orange and Pomegranate Salad*	• 2 boiled eggs with wholemeal roll and spread OR • Home made porridge OR • 2 Weetabix with raisins WITH • Granary toast and spread PLUS • Strawberry smoothie	• *Mexican Brunch* OR • *Dried Fruit Salad* OR • Croissant with jam and clementine PLUS • Skinny cappuccino	• Muesli with yogurt and raspberries OR • Bran flakes with ready-to-eat apricots OR • Currant bun with spread and banana PLUS • Mango and peach smoothie
• *Barley and Roasted Vegetable Salad with Pumpkins Seeds* OR • *Bean and Salsa Wrap* OR • Scrambled egg on toast with grilled tomatoes	• *Moroccan Hummus with Flatbread* OR • *Quinoa, Feta and Spinach Salad* OR • Cheddar and tomato sandwich in sunflower seed roll • *Citrus Salad Bowl*	• Bought 'healthier' vegetable pizza OR • Smoked salmon and cream cheese bagel OR • *Sardine and Cheese Toastie* • Greek yogurt with strawberries and honey OR • Fresh mango	• *Home-made Fish Goujons with Piquant Avocado Dip* OR • *Baba Ganoush with Bread and Asparagus Tips* WITH • *Sardine and Pepper Strudels* OR • *Tzatziki with Raw Vegetables* AND • *Two Pear Salad* OR • *Patatas Bravas* • Papaya with lime juice OR • *Summer Fruit Compote* (with xylitol)
• *Tuna Steak with Sundried Tomato Crust and Lime Dressing* OR • *Pot Roasted Lamb Shanks* OR • *Stuffed Portobello Mushrooms* WITH • *Gratin of Potato* OR • Plain cooked pasta AND • *Spinach with Currants and Pinenuts* OR • Green salad with dressing • Slice of Galia melon OR • 2 Kiwi fruit	• Watercress soup • *Steak and Broccoli with Noodles* OR • *Asparagus risotto* OR • *Italian Chicken Gnocchi* • *Chocolate Brioche Pudding* OR • *Honey-roasted Stone Fruit*	• *Tarka Dhal* WITH • *Almond Rice* OR • *Salmon and Asparagus en Croûte* WITH • *Hot Potato Salad* OR • *Teriyaki Turkey* WITH • *Quinoa and Sunflower Seeds* AND • *Curly Kale with Garlic Cherry Tomatoes* OR • Peas and carrots • *Strawberry Mousse* OR • *Citrus Salad Bowl*	• *Crab Linguine* OR • *Baked Beef and Sour Cherries* WITH brown rice OR • *Butternut Squash Bake with Halloumi and Pomegranate* WITH • Watercress and orange salad OR • Peas and carrots OR • Green salad with dressing • *Apple and Blackcurrant Oat Crumble* OR • *Traditional Rice Pudding*
• Glass of milk • *Orange Bran Muffin*	• Mango OR papaya • *Fruity Flapjack*	• 25 g chocolate Brazil nuts	• 55 g dried fruit, nuts and seeds • Fruit yogurt

NOTES: Portion of vegetables or fruit is 80 g or more unless specified. Where lower fat options exist assume these are used. All spread assumed to be reduced fat (60%) olive spread. Yogurt is low fat unless stated. Mayonnaise is 3% fat and 1 tbsp only is used in sandwiches. Bread is an average slice of 32 g, 2 slices per sandwich. Salad dressing is assumed to be 1 tbsp standard French dressing.

		Monday	Tuesday	Wednesday
breakfast		• *Porridge with Raspberries and Walnuts* OR • *Citrus Salad Bowl* OR • Bran flakes with apricots • Pineapple based smoothie	• Scrambled egg with tomatoes and toast OR • Muesli with blueberries OR • *Berry Yogurt Greakfast* • Apple OR orange juice	• *Berry Yogurt Breakfast* OR • Boiled eggs with marmite on toast OR • *Orange Bran Muffin* WITH • Glass of milk AND • *Citrus Salad Bowl*
lunch		• Peanut butter and watercress sandwich OR • *Beef and Beet Sandwich* OR • *Quinoa, Feta and Spinach Salad* • 1 orange OR some mango cubes	• Baked beans on 2 pieces toast OR • Greens soup with cheese roll OR • *Smoked Mackerel, Ricotta and Beetroot Bruschetta* • Half papaya with lime juice OR • Large kiwi fruit	• *Sardine and Cheese Toastie* OR • Baked potato with tuna OR • *Bean and Salsa Wrap* WITH • Green salad and dressing • Grapes OR ready-to-eat prunes
dinner		• *Crab Linguine* OR • *Aparagus Risotto* OR • *Jambalaya* WITH • Green salad with dressing OR • Green beans and chorizo • *Chocolate Brazil Brownie* OR • *Honey-roasted Stone Fruit*	• *Tuna Steak with Sundried Tomato Crust and Lime Dressing* OR • *Duck with Cherry Sauce and Leek Mash* OR • *Brazil Nut Burger* in bun WITH • *Kachumbari* OR • *Roast Beetroot and Butternut Squash* AND • *Orange and Mint Cous cous* OR • *Hot Potato Salad* • *Strawberry Mousse* OR • *Mango and Lime Dessert*	• *Butternut Squash Bake with Halloumi and Pomegranate* OR • *Pork and Roasted Vegetable Tray Bake* OR • *Duck with Cherry Sauce and Leek Mash* WITH • *Green Chilli Edamame* OR • *Curly Kale with Garlic Cherry Tomatoes* • *Pear in Chocolate Sauce* OR • *Raspberry and Pomegranate Jelly*
snacks		• Fruit yogurt • *Fruity Flapjack*	• *Carrot Tray Bake*	• *Cheddar and Sundried Tomato Scone*

DRINKS: 300 ml semi-skimmed milk or fortified soya equivalent in drinks throughout the day. Water ad lib throughout the day, and herb tea, coffee and tea as guided by chapter 3. Fruit juice assumed to be 200 ml glass unsweetened.

Thursday	Friday	Saturday	Sunday
• Mango, apricot and pineapple smoothie with currant bread OR • *Orange Bran Muffin* WITH • Glass of milk OR • *Raspberry Porridge with Walnuts*	• *Raisin and Apple Pancakes* OR • Weetabix with raisins OR • Muesli with blueberries AND • Berry smoothie	• Croissant and jam with clementines OR • *Orange Bran Muffin* WITH • Glass of milk OR • *Raspberry Porridge with Walnuts*	• *Mexican Brunch* OR • Weetabix with raisins OR • *Raspberry Porridge with Walnuts* AND • Orange juice
• *Barley and Roasted Vegetable Salad with Pumpkins Seeds* OR • *Beef and Beet Sandwich* OR • Carrot and coriander soup and wholemeal roll • Apple juice	• *Crab Cakes with Watercress and Orange Salad* OR • *Mushroom and Asparagus Omelette* OR • *Ratatouille with Halloumi and Bread* WITH • *Chilli Edamame and Peppers* OR • *Cucumber and Sesame Salad*	• *Stuffed Portobello Mushrooms* OR • *Watercress and salmon salad* OR • *Baba Ganoush with Bread and Asparagus Tips* WITH • Green salad and dressing • Slice of melon or an apple	• Greens soup with cheese roll OR • Boiled eggs with wholemeal roll OR • *Sardine and Cheese Toastie* WITH • Cherry tomatoes • *Fruity Flapjack* OR • *Carrot Tray Bake*
• *Sprats with avocado and Tomato Salad* OR • *Beef in Beer* OR • *Spinach Stuffed Chicken Breast with Proscuitto* WITH • *Herbed Barley* OR • *Leek Mash* AND • *Spinach with Currants and Pnenuts* • *Summer Fruit Compote* OR • Plums	• *Water Chestnut and Cashew Nut Stir Fry* OR • *Chorizo and Black Eyed Beans with Giant Cous cous* OR • *Paella* WITH • Sweetcorn AND • Broccoli with Almonds and Sundried Tomatoes • *Pear in Chocolate Sauce* OR • *Chocolate Brazil Brownie*	• *Black Eye Beans, Currant and Fresh Mint Stew* OR • *Sea Bass with Pomegranate Salsa* OR • *Hungarian Goulash* WITH • New potatoes OR • Brown rice AND • *Roasted Beetroot and Butternut Squash* OR • *Broccoli with Amonds* • *Orange and Pomegranate Salad* OR • Greek yogurt, blueberries and honey	• *Pot Roasted Lamb Shanks* OR • *Roasted Baby Vegetables with Tofu* OR • *Tuna Steak with Sundried Tomato Crust and Lime Dressing* WITH • *Hot Potato Salad* OR • *Gratin of Potato* AND • Purple sprouting broccoli • Tropical fruit salad OR • Yogurt with blueberries • Raspberries
• Chocolate digestive biscuit	• Grapes OR Kiwi fruit • Chocolate Brazils	• Mango and passion fruit smoothie	• Ready-to-eat prunes • *Cheddar and Sundried Tomato Scone*

NOTES: Portion of vegetables or fruit is 80 g or more unless specified. Where lower fat options exist assume these are used. All spread assumed to be reduced fat (60%) olive spread. Yogurt is low fat unless stated. Mayonnaise is 3% fat and 1 tbsp only is used in sandwiches. Bread is an average slice of 32 g, 2 slices per sandwich. Salad dressing is assumed to be 1 tbsp standard French dressing.

THIRD TRIMESTER

		Monday	Tuesday	Wednesday
breakfast		• 2 boiled eggs with wholemeal toast OR • Bran flakes with ready-to-eat apricots OR • 2 wheat biscuits with blueberries • Glass of orange juice	• Muesli with blueberries OR • 2 wheat biscuits with raisins OR • 2 boiled eggs with marmite on toast • Glass of orange juice	• Smoked salmon and cream cheese bagel OR • *Raspberry Porridge with Walnuts* OR • Cheerios • Glass of orange juice
lunch		• Scrambled egg with grilled tomatoes and toast OR • Baked potato with tuna OR • Cheddar and tomato sunflower seed roll • 2 clemetines AND • 1 fruit yogurt	• *Home-made Fish Goujons with Piquant Avocado Dip* OR • *Roasted Red Pepper Paté* with granary bread OR • Smoked mackerel paté and cucumber sandwich • *Carrot Tray Bake*	• Peanut butter and watercress sandwich OR • Prawn and cucumber sandwich OR • Mushroom soup with a few chopped walnuts and a wholemeal roll • Greek yogurt with strawberries and honey AND • 1 chocolate digestive biscuit
dinner		• *Mushroom-stuffed Chicken with Puy Lentils* OR • *Crab Cakes with Watercress and Orange Salad* OR • *Brazil Nut Burger* in a roll WITH • *Ginger and Orange Slaw* OR • *Roasted Beetroot and Butternut Squash* AND • *Orange and Mint Cous cous* • 2 scoops ice cream OR • 1 scoop with *Summer Fruit Compote*	• *Greek Style Tomato and Haddock* OR • *Pork with Pineapple* OR • *Black Eye Bean, Currant and Fresh Mint Stew* WITH • *Leek Mash* OR • *Almond Rice* AND • *Watercress and Orange Salad* OR • *Broccoli with Almonds* • *Traditional Rice Pudding* OR • *Baked Fig with Pistachios and Honey Yogurt*	• *Pasta Primavera* OR • *Tuna and Vegetable Pasta Bake* OR • *Italian Chicken Gnocchi* WITH • Broccoli or carrots • *Strawberry Mousse*
snacks		• 25g bag low fat crisps • *Cheddar and Sundried Tomato Scone* • *Fruity Flapjack*	• Glass of milk • *Chocolate Brazil Brownie*	• Glass of milk • *Fruity Flapjack*

DRINKS: 300 ml semi-skimmed milk or fortified soya equivalent in drinks throughout the day. Water ad lib throughout the day, and herb tea, coffee and tea as guided by chapter 3. Fruit juice assumed to be 200 ml glass unsweetened.

Thursday	Friday	Saturday	Sunday
• Shredded wheat with strawberries OR • *Orange Bran Muffin* WITH • Glass of milk OR • Croissant and jam WITH • Clementine	• Greek yogurt, blueberries and honey OR • Croissant and jam WITH • Clementine OR • Bran flakes with sultanas • Berry smoothie OR • Chai masala	• Grilled bacon, tomatoes and mushrooms OR • *Orange Bran Muffin* AND • Glass of milk OR • *Raspberry Porridge with Walnuts* AND • Slice of toast and spread • Glass of orange juice	• *Mexican Brunch* OR • Shredded wheat with strawberries OR • Croissant and jam WITH • Clementine • ½ grapefruit
• *Morrocan Hummus with Flatbread* OR • Home-made vegetable pizza OR • Ham salad sandwich with seeded bread • 2 kiwi fruit or 3 plums	• *Sardine and Pepper Strudel* OR • 2 boiled eggs with marmite on toast OR • Turkey and cranberry salad sandwich AND • Yogurt with berries OR • Papaya with lime • *Chocolate Brazil Brownie*	• *Smoked Mackerel, Ricotta and Beetroot Bruschetta* OR • *Cos, Chicken and Croûtons Salad* OR • 2 boiled eggs with marmite on toast • Mango cubes OR • 3 ready-to-eat apricots	• Carrot and coriander soup with a roll OR • Smoked salmon and cream cheese bagel OR • *Moroccan Houmous with Flatbread* WITH • Green salad
• *Stuffed Portobello Mushrooms* OR • *Baked Beef and Sour Cherries* OR • *Greek Style Tomato and Haddock* WITH • *Hot Potato Salad* OR • *Tabbouleh with Pine Nuts* AND • *Two Pear Salad* • *Pear in Chocolate Sauce* OR • *Raisin and Apple Pancake*	• *Smoked Salmon Flakes with Herbed Lentils* OR • *Duck and Oriental Mushroom Stir Fry* OR • *Water Chestnut and Cashew Stir Fry* • *Strawberry Mousse* OR • *Mango and Lime Dessert*	• *Beef in Beer* OR • *Lamb and Pepper Koftas with Tzatziki* OR • *Mushroom and Asparagus Omelette* WITH • *Gratin of Potato* OR • Pasta AND • *Broccoli with Almonds* OR • *Spinach with Currants and Pine Nuts*	• Duck with *Cherry Sauce and Leek Mash* OR • *Moroccan Lamb Tagine* OR • *Roasted Baby Vegetables with Tofu* WITH • *Orange and Mint Cous cous* AND • Peas AND • *Curly Kale with Garlic Cherry Tomatoes* • *Traditional Rice Pudding* OR • 2 scoops ice cream
• *Cheddar and Sundried Tomato Scone* • Glass of orange juice	• Cappuccino • *Moroccan Hummus with Flatbread*	• Greek yogurt and blueberries • Hot spicy apple drink	• Glass of milk • Pineapple, banana and ginger smoothie

NOTES: Portion of vegetables or fruit is 80 g or more unless specified. Where lower fat options exist assume these are used. All spread assumed to be reduced fat (60%) olive spread. Yogurt is low fat unless stated. Mayonnaise is 3% fat and 1 tbsp only is used in sandwiches. Bread is an average slice of 32 g, 2 slices per sandwich. Salad dressing is assumed to be 1 tbsp standard French dressing.
1 tbsp standard French dressing.

NEWBORN WEEKS

	Monday	Tuesday	Wednesday
breakfast	• Oatibix flakes with dried fruit OR • *Raspberry Porridge with Walnuts* OR • *Mexican Brunch*	• *Orange bran muffin* OR • Weetabix with blueberries OR • Boiled eggs with wholemeal roll • Orange juice	• *Raisin and apple pancakes* OR • *Raspberry Porridge with Walnuts* OR • Muesli with blueberries • Orange juice
lunch	• Baked potato with tuna mayo OR • *Sardine and Cheese Toastie* OR • *Beef and Beet Sandwich* • Banana or dried apricots	• Carrot soup with roll OR • *Tuna and Vegetabe Pasta Bake* OR • Scrambled eggs with grilled tomato and toast • Apple	• *Smoked Salmon Flakes with Herbed Lentils* OR • *Sardine and Cheese Toastie* OR • *Moroccan Houmous and Flatbread* • 2 clementines
dinner	• *Sweet Potato and Chestnut Jalousie* OR • *Moroccan Lamb Tagine* OR • *Salmon en Croûte* WITH • *Orange and Mint Cous cous* OR • *Hot Potato Salad* AND • *Watercress and Orange Salad* AND • *Curly Kale with Garlic Cherry Tomatoes* • *Traditional Rice Pudding*	• *Crab Linguine* OR • *Mushroom and Asparagus Omelette* OR • *Mushroom-stuffed Chicken with Puy Lentils* WITH • Mashed potato AND • Peas and carrots OR • *Green Beans with Chorizo* • *Raspberry and Pomegranate Jelly* OR • *Apple and Blackcurrant Oat Crumble*	• *Teriyaki Turkey with Sesame Cucumber Salad* OR • *Tuna Steak with Tomato Crust and Lime Dressing* OR • *Tarka Dhal* WITH • *Almond Rice* AND • *Spinach with Currants and Pine Nuts* OR • *Watercress and Orange Salad* • *Pear in Chocolate Sauce* OR • 2 scoops ice cream
snacks	• Berry smoothie • *Chocolate Brazil Brownie*	• Fruit yogurt • *Fruity flapjack*	• Fruit yogurt

DRINKS: 300 ml semi-skimmed milk or fortified soya equivalent in drinks throughout the day. Water ad lib throughout the day, and herb tea, coffee and tea as guided by chapter 3. Fruit juice assumed to be 200 ml glass unsweetened.

Thursday	Friday	Saturday	Sunday
• Tropical smoothie with currant bread OR • Oatibix flakes with dried fruit OR • 2 hot cross buns	• *Mexican Brunch* OR • Boiled eggs with wholemeal toast OR • Oatibix flakes with dried fruit • Orange juice	• *Orange Bran Muffin* WITH • milk OR • Weetabix with raisins OR • *Mushroom and Asparagus Omelette*	• Bran flakes with dried apricots OR • 2 slices wholemeal toast WITH chopped banana OR • Croissant and jam WITH • 2 clementines
• *Barley and Roasted Vegetable Salad* OR • *Crab Cakes with Watercress and Orange Salad* • Fresh mango AND • *Fruity Flapjack*	• *Beef and Beet Sandwich* OR • *Red Pepper Paté* WITH toast and salad AND • 30 g bag roasted vegetable crisps	• *Cos, Chicken and Croûtons* OR • *Crab Cakes with Watercress and Orange Salad* OR • *Baba Ganoush with Bread and Asparagus Tips* • Fruit yogurt	• *Beef and Beet Sandwich* OR • *Brazil Nut Burger* in a bun OR • *Sardine and Cheese Toastie*
• *Pea and Spinach Soup* AND • *Chinese Beef and Noodles* OR • *Jambalaya* OR • *Wild Rice Pilaf with Haddock, Peas and Capers* • Fruit yogurt	• *Brazil Nut Burgers* in a bun OR • *Tarka Dhal* WITH naan bread OR • *Paella* WITH • *Broccoli and Almonds* OR • *Curly Kale with Garlic Cherry Tomatoes* • Greek yogurt WITH strawberries and honey OR • *Chocolate Brioche Pudding*	• *Pork with Plums* OR • *Tuna Steak with Sundried Tomato Crust and Lime Dressing* OR • *Creamy Vegetarian Mince* WITH • *Almond rice* AND • *Green Chilli Edamame* OR • *Ginger and Orange Slaw* • *Honey and Pistachio Fig with Yogurt* OR • *Mango and Lime Dessert*	• *Crab Cake with Watercress and Orange Salad* OR • *Sesame Chicken with Mango Salsa* OR • *Stuffed Portobello Mushrooms* WITH • *Quinoa and Sunflower Seeds* OR • *Leek mash* AND • *Curly Kale with Garlic Cherry Tomatoes* OR • Green salad with dressing • *Raisin and Apple Pancake* OR • Greek yogurt with blueberries and honey
• *Chocolate Brazil Brownie*	• 3-4 chocolate Brazil nuts	• *Cheddar and Sundried Tomato Scone*	• *Carrot Tray Bake* OR • *Summer Fruit Compote* and ice cream

NOTES: Portion of vegetables or fruit is 80 g or more unless specified. Where lower fat options exist assume these are used. All spread assumed to be reduced fat (60%) olive spread. Yogurt is low fat unless stated. Mayonnaise is 3% fat and 1 tbsp only is used in sandwiches. Bread is an average slice of 32 g, 2 slices per sandwich. Salad dressing is assumed to be 1 tbsp standard French dressing.

CHAPTER 5

RECIPES

citrus salad bowl

- -

Vitamin C is vital in protecting you and your baby from infection. Citrus fruits and kiwi are amongst the highest providers of this vitamin and make a colourful breakfast salad.

- -
serves 2
preparation time 5 minutes
cooking time 0 minutes
- -

1 medium grapefruit, colour of your choice
2 seedless clementines
1 large or 2 small kiwi fruit

1 Peel the grapefruit with a sharp knife, then, holding the fruit over a mixing bowl to catch any juice, cut away each segment from the membrane. Add to the bowl.
2 Peel the clementines and separate into segments and add to the bowl.
3 Peel the kiwi fruit and cut into rounds. Stir into the bowl and serve the fruit salad at once.

serving suggestions
Top with toasted almonds or seeds, and yogurt, and follow with toast, muffins or porridge.

storage
The fruit salad can be stored for 24 hours in an airtight container in the fridge but is not suitable for freezing.

raspberry porridge with walnuts

- -

Oats promote heart health and are also great for keeping hunger at bay and this hot breakfast will keep you going all morning.

- -
serves 1
preparation time 2 minutes
cooking time 5 minutes
- -

40 g quick cook oatmeal/rolled oats
250 ml semi-skimmed milk
30 g frozen raspberries
1 tbsp maple syrup
10 g walnuts (approx. 3 walnut halves)

1 Place the oatmeal and milk in a small saucepan and bring to simmering point stirring frequently.
2 Once it has thickened, remove from the heat and add the raspberries. Allow to stand for a few seconds before stirring in the berries, then pour oatmeal into a serving dish.
3 Top with the maple syrup and walnuts.

serving suggestions
Eat with a hot drink or a glass of fruit juice.

allergens
Gluten (oats), milk, nuts (walnuts).

> **COOK'S TIP**
> *Frozen raspberries are much cheaper than fresh and quickly defrost in the porridge.*

raisin and apple pancakes

Ring the changes from toast and marmalade by making these fruity pancakes. They make a great weekend brunch when you may have a little more time to cook, and there will be some left over to freeze for other, more rushed, mornings. Nutritionally they provide bone-building magnesium and calcium, B vitamins and zinc, as well as one fifth of your iron needs.

serves 4
preparation time 10 minutes
cooking time 15-20 minutes

125 g wholemeal flour
125 g plain white flour
3 tsp baking powder
1 tsp ground cinnamon
2 medium eggs
250 ml semi-skimmed milk
2 tbsp maple syrup
1 medium cooking apple
   (you need 100 g grated apple)
75 g raisins

Rapeseed oil for cooking
Plain yogurt, to serve

1 Preheat your oven to 110°C, 90°C for fan ovens or gas mark ¼.
2 Sieve the flours, baking powder and cinnamon into a large mixing bowl, adding in any bran which remains.
3 Add the eggs, milk and syrup and, using a hand mixer or blender, combine to make a thick batter.
4 Peel the apple and grate coarsely, and add approximately 100g of apple to the batter along with the raisins. Stir well to combine.
5 Using a medium-to-high flame or hob temperature, heat a griddle or non-stick frying pan until hot and add half a teaspoon of oil.
6 Pour a ladleful of batter onto the frying pan and allow it to spread. When it is just golden brown on the base, carefully turn it over with a spatula or palette knife and allow to cook on the other side. This will probably take 2-3 minutes per side, depending on your cooker. The thicker the mixture, the lower the heat will need to be, to ensure the inside is cooked.
7 Once the pancake is ready, remove from the pan and keep warm in the oven whilst you cook the remaining batter. Or, if you are keeping some for another day, allow to cool.
8 Serve the pancakes whilst still warm.

serving suggestions
Accompany each pancake with 1 tbsp plain yogurt. You could also try a spoonful of maple syrup, fresh fruit or Summer Fruit Compote, page 142.

storage
The pancakes are ideal for freezing, so when you have made a batch, using interleaving sheets or greaseproof paper to keep separate, and place in an airtight container. Freeze for up to 3 months. You can remove individual pancakes and defrost and reheat in a microwave cooker.

allergens
Gluten (wheat), eggs, milk (milk and yogurt).

berry yogurt breakfast

Make this colourful berry dish a regular part of your morning as it provides all your day's vitamin C and 40% of your calcium requirements. The sunflower seeds also provide protective zinc and vitamin E.

serves 1
preparation time 5 minutes
cooking time 0 minutes

150 g carton fat-free plain yogurt
50 g strawberries, hulled and halved
50 g raspberries
1 teaspoon runny honey
1 tbsp sunflower seeds, toasted

1 Spoon the yogurt into the serving bowl and top with the fruit.
2 Drizzle over the honey and lastly sprinkle the seeds on top.

serving suggestions
Follow with a wholemeal English muffin and a glass of juice.

storage
This is not suitable for storage.

allergens
Milk (yogurt).

Mexican brunch

Not only tasty and filling, this Mexican-style dish provides one quarter of your day's need for iron, vitamin C, and folic acid as well as being a source of fibre. So tuck in, safe in the knowledge you and your baby are being well nourished!

serves 1
preparation time 15 minutes
cooking time 15 minutes

for the tomato salsa
1 large ripe tomato at room temperature
1 tbsp tomato chutney or relish
1 tsp chopped coriander (optional)

for the scrambled eggs
1 medium free range egg
2 tbsp semi skimmed milk
black pepper (optional)
1 tsp reduced fat polyunsaturated spread

2 heaped tbsp cooked black beans (see box right)
1 corn or wholemeal tortilla wrap

1 Preheat your oven to 110°C, 90°C for fan oven or gas mark ¼, and place a plate to warm along with the tortilla wrapped in foil.
2 Cut the tomato into small pieces and mix with the chutney or relish and coriander, if used.
3 Beat the egg it in a small bowl with the milk and pepper. Melt the spread in a small saucepan and pour in the egg mixture. Cook over a low heat, stirring frequently until the egg just sets.
4 Meanwhile, heat the beans in a small saucepan, adding a little water to prevent sticking, if required.
5 Remove the tortilla and warmed plate from the oven and serve the beans, salsa and egg with the tortilla.

serving suggestions
Accompany with a glass of fruit juice or a smoothie.

allergens
Gluten (wheat), egg, milk.

> **COOK'S TIP**
> *Look out for cans of black beans (sometimes called turtle beans) in water in supermarkets. Alternatively, buy dried black beans. It is worth preparing at least 250 g of dried beans at once as the cooked beans will freeze well for up to 3 months. Simply soak the dried beans overnight and then cook according to packet instructions.*

mushroom and asparagus omelette

Whether you fancy something special for Sunday brunch or want a quick supper or tasty lunch, this omelette ticks many of your nutritional requirement boxes, as well as tasting great. Just make sure to cook the eggs until they are firm, popping under a hot grill if necessary to set the top.

serves 2
preparation time 10 minutes
cooking time 10 minutes

1 tbsp vegetable oil
200g closed cup mushrooms, sliced
200g fresh asparagus
4 large free range eggs
Pinch salt and little black pepper
1 tsp vegetable oil

1 Heat the oil in a non stick pan and gently fry the mushrooms, stirring often for 3-4 minutes. Cover.

2 Meanwhile, slice off the bottom 1cm of the asparagus stalks and discard. Then cut off the tip along with 5-6 cm of each stalk, and place on one side. Slice the remaining stalk into 1-cm pieces, and cook with the mushrooms until just tender, around 10 minutes.

3 Whilst the mushrooms cook, steam the remaining asparagus tips until just tender using a basket steamer, a saucepan (see page 80) or purpose-made asparagus steamer.

4 Beat the eggs with the seasoning and 1 tbsp water.

5 Heat the oil in a non-stick omelette pan over a medium heat and pour in the egg. When the base is beginning to set, move this to the centre, allowing the runny egg to spread to the edges. Repeat once or twice until the egg is set.

6 Fill the set omelette with the mushroom filling, tip carefully onto a warmed plate and cut in half.

7 Serve each half with half the asparagus tips on the side.

serving suggestions
Accompany with fresh crusty bread, and a few cherry tomatoes.   .

allergens
Eggs.

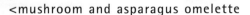

<mushroom and asparagus omelette

baba ganoush with bread and asparagus tips

This aubergine dip is found in many countries in the Middle East, and is simple to make. Served with folate-rich asparagus tips and some wholemeal pitta, it makes a delicious snack which provides more than a quarter of your pregnancy needs for iron, zinc and folate. Or, you can make a meal of it by serving alongside some grilled lamb chops and Tzatziki (see page 00).

serves 2
preparation time   10 minutes
cooking time   25 minutes

1 medium aubergine
1 tbsp tahini paste
1 clove garlic, crushed
2 tsp lemon juice
1 tbsp flat-leaved parsley, chopped
black pepper

to serve
100 g asparagus tips, lightly steamed
2 wholemeal pitta, toasted

1 Preheat the grill to high, and the oven to 200°C, 180°C for fan oven or gas mark 6.
2 Cut the aubergine in half and place flesh side down under the grill until the skin starts to blacken.
3 Remove and pop in the oven until the flesh is very tender — about 10–20 minutes depending on how well grilled the aubergine was. Allow to cool.
4 Scoop out the flesh from the aubergine halves and place in a small bowl or blender bowl.
5 Add the tahini, garlic and lemon juice and blend until smooth.
6 Quickly blend in the parsley and black pepper.
7 Serve with the steamed asparagus and wholemeal pitta bread.

storage
Baba ganoush can be stored in the fridge for up to 48 hours but is not suitable for freezing.

allergens
Wheat (gluten), sesame.

green beans and chorizo

This supremely simple dish based on a Spanish tapa uses spicy chorizo (best bought in a block from the deli), but you could use salami if you prefer. It is rich in energy-releasing vitamin B_1, as well as zinc and vitamin B_{12} — both essential pregnancy nutrients.

serves 2
preparation time 5 minutes
cooking time 0 minutes

270 g stringless flat green beans such as helda or
   runner beans, cut into 2–3 cm pieces
100 g chorizo, cut into small cubes
1 tbsp olive oil mixed with 1 tbsp lemon juice

1 Steam the beans until just tender.
2 Cook the chorizo in a dry pan, allowing the juices to flow out.
3 Add the chorizo to the beans and mix, then stir in the olive oil and lemon juice.

serving suggestions
Eat with crusty bread or another tapas-style dish such as Patatas Bravas, page 60.

allergens
Chorizo may contain milk, sulphites and wheat.

bruschettas

The classic topping for these snacks is fresh tomatoes, but there are many variations you can make, which will not only provide interest but will boost some key pregnancy nutrients. The smoked mackerel, ricotta and beetroot version makes a really healthy and colourful lunch or snack as it provides omega 3 fatty acids and vitamins D and B$_{12}$.

tomato, basil and mozzarella

serves 2
preparation time 5 minutes
cooking time 0 minutes

2 medium tomatoes, quartered and seeds removed
pinch salt
black pepper
2–3 large basil leaves, roughly torn
1 tbsp olive oil
2 slices bruschettina or 2 x 1 cm slices of a large
   ciabatta
1 clove garlic, peeled
50 g fresh mozzarella, cut into cubes

1 Roughly chop the tomatoes, and mix with the salt, pepper, basil and olive oil. Leave to infuse for a few minutes.
2 Meanwhile, toast the bruschettina and scrape the garlic clove over the bread.
3 Spoon over the topping and add a the cubes of mozzarella.

allergens
Wheat (gluten) , milk (mozzarella).

STORAGE
The completed bruschettas should be eaten right away, but each of the toppings can be kept in the fridge for up to 24 hours.

roasted pepper and olive

serves 2
preparation time 5 minutes
cooking time 30 minutes

½ medium red and ½ medium green pepper, cut into large chunks
2 tsp olive oil
2 slices bruschettina or 2 x 1 cm slices of a large ciabatta
30 g pitted black olives in brine, drained and sliced
2 tsp sundried tomato paste

1 Preheat an oven to 200°C, 180°C for fan oven or gas mark 6.
2 Place the peppers in a small roasting or ovenproof dish and drizzle with the oil.
3 Roast for 25–30 minutes, turning occasionally to coat in the oil, until the peppers are softened.
4 Allow to cool, and chop roughly into smaller pieces.
5 Lightly toast the bread and spread each slice with the sundried tomato paste.
6 Mix the peppers with the black olives and spoon on to the bread.

allergens
Wheat (gluten).

smoked mackerel, ricotta and beetroot

serves 3
preparation time 15 minutes
cooking time 0 minutes

1 fillet smoked mackerel (around 75 g)
1 tbsp lemon juice
50g ricotta
1 tsp hot horseradish
1 tbsp parsley, finely chopped
50 g cooked beetroot, roughly chopped
3 slices bruschettina or 3 x 1 cm slices of a large ciabatta
olive oil

1 Remove the skin from the mackerel and discard.
2 Place the mackerel and lemon juice in a mixing bowl and using a fork, break up the fish.
3 Add the ricotta, horseradish and parsley and mix until smooth.
4 Mix in the cooked beetroot.
5 Meanwhile, toast the bread and drizzle with a little olive oil. Top with the fish mixture.

allergens
Wheat (gluten), milk (ricotta).

patatas bravas

Even taking into account nutrients lost through cooking, this dish is rich in vitamin C and very simple to make. The tomato sauce is a pregnancy basic, so it's well worth making double the quantity you need and freezing half. This can then be used to accompany meat, chicken or fish, or served with pasta.

serves 4 as a starter
preparation time 15 minutes
cooking time 40–50 minutes

for the potatoes
650 g roasting potatoes such as Maris Piper or King Edward, scrubbed and cut into 2-cm cubes
2 tbsp vegetable oil

for the tomato sauce
1 tbsp olive oil
1 medium onion (160 g), finely chopped
2 cloves garlic, crushed
1 tsp paprika (optional)
1 tsp chilli powder (optional)
400 g can chopped tomatoes in tomato juice
2 tbsp tomato purée
pinch sugar
black pepper

to serve
2 tbsp parsley, chopped

COOK'S TIP
There's no need to peel the potatoes, just make sure they are well scrubbed.

1 Preheat the oven to 200°C, 180°C for fan oven or gas mark 6.
2 Place the oil in a roasting tin and heat in the oven until hot.
3 Tip in the potatoes and turn them to coat in the oil.
4 Roast the potatoes, turning occasionally until golden and crisp, about 40–50 minutes.
5 Meanwhile prepare the sauce by heating the oil in a non-stick saucepan and frying the onion until softened.
6 Add the garlic, spices if using, canned tomatoes and purée, and stir in the sugar.
7 Bring to the boil, stirring, and then simmer for 10–15 minutes until the sauce is pulpy and soft.
8 Season to taste with black pepper.
9 When the potatoes are cooked, place in a serving dish and cover with the sauce. Sprinkle with the chopped parsley.

serving suggestions
Eat with other little plates as part of a tapas-style meal or as an accompaniment to a main-course dish.

storage
The sauce can be stored in an airtight container in the fridge for up to 48 hours. Alternatively the sauce can be frozen and reheated until piping hot.

VARIATION
Omit the spices from the sauce and add your favourite herbs, or drop in a few black olives and some lemon zest, or add some chopped red or yellow bell pepper.

little bites

60

mediterranean vegetable parcels

Just one of these tasty parcels provides half of the vitamin C you need each day in pregnancy, but you may well be tempted to eat two as a main course. Just add some couscous or tabbouleh and a tomato salad for a great meal.

serves 4
preparation time 10 minutes
cooking time 25 minutes

1 medium courgette
½ medium red pepper
½ medium yellow pepper
1 small red onion, finely chopped
1 tbsp oregano, freshly chopped
1 tbsp mint, freshly chopped
100 g feta cheese, cut into cubes
black pepper
8 sheets filo pastry
2 tbsp vegetable oil

1 Preheat the oven to 200°C, 180°C for fan oven or gas mark 6.
2 Cut the courgette and peppers into 1-cm dice and place in a bowl. Add the chopped onion and herbs and mix well.
3 Add the feta and grind over some black pepper.
4 Place the filo pastry on a board and brush or spray the top piece with oil.
5 Spoon one quarter of the vegetable mixture into the centre and wrap to make a rectangular parcel.
6 Brush another sheet with oil and wrap the parcel again, this time placing the thicker layer on top. Place on to a baking sheet lined with non-stick paper or baking parchment.
7 Make another three parcels.
8 Lightly brush or spray the finished parcels with oil and bake for 25 minutes or until golden brown.

serving suggestions
The parcels can be eaten hot or at room temperature accompanied by a side salad and some bread, or by Tabbouleh with Pine Nuts, page 64.

storage
For maximum vitamin C content, serve these parcels on the day they are made, but they can be stored in the fridge for up to 48 hours and reheated until piping hot.

allergens
Wheat (gluten), milk (feta cheese).

VARIATION
Use finely chopped aubergine, cherry tomatoes and a few olives or capers instead of the courgette or peppers.

little bites

roasted red pepper pâté

This delicious vegetarian pâté is not only full of finely flavoured ingredients, but it's a wonderful way of getting plenty of vitamins C and A. It makes a great lunch with crusty bread and a mixed salad, or can be served alongside some of the other little dishes in this section.

serves 4
preparation time 10 minutes
cooking time 30 minutes

2 red bell peppers, cut into large chunks
½ red onion, peeled and chopped
2 tbsp olive oil
5 large fresh basil leaves, torn into 2 or 3 pieces
1 clove garlic, peeled and chopped
100 g mascarpone cheese
1 tsp sundried tomato purée
2 tsp lemon juice
black pepper, to taste

1 Preheat the oven to 200°C,180°C for fan oven or gas mark 6.
2 Place the peppers and onion in a roasting tin, drizzle over the oil and roast in the oven for 30 minutes, or until the peppers are soft.
3 Allow to cool for a few minutes, then transfer the mixture to a food processor. Add the basil and pulse lightly to mix. Add the remaining ingredients and pulse again until smooth.
4 Spoon the pâté into individual ramekins or one large dish. Chill before serving.

serving suggestions
Eat on toasted walnut or seed bread alongside a crisp green salad.

storage
The pâté can be stored in an airtight container in the fridge for up to 48 hours but is not suitable for freezing.

allergens
Milk.

tzatziki with raw vegetables

It's not so much the dip, but the vegetables which give this simple snack its high nutritional value. Cauliflower, baby corn and carrot provide essential vitamins A, C and folate, and since they are eaten raw, cooking losses are vastly reduced. The Greek yogurt also contains valuable calcium and riboflavin and the quantities are similar whether you choose 0 per cent fat yogurt as specified, or go for one that has a 2 or 10 per cent fat content.

serves 2
preparation time 20 minutes

7-cm cucumber (approx 100 g)
salt
150 g fat-free Greek yogurt
1 tbsp extra virgin olive oil
1 tbsp mint, chopped
1 medium carrot, scrubbed and sliced into batons
2 florets cauliflower, cut into smaller pieces
50 g baby sweetcorn, washed and steamed, if you prefer

optional extras
1 clove garlic, crushed
Zest of 1 lemon
Dill, to replace mint, if preferred

1 Wash the cucumber and slice lengthwise. Scoop out the seeds, and chop into small pieces.
2 Place in a colander or on some kitchen paper and sprinkle with a pinch or two of salt. Allow to stand for 10–15 minutes to allow some water to drain from the cucumber.
3 Meanwhile mix the yogurt with the oil and mint.
4 Pat dry the cucumber, wiping away any excess salt and mix into the yogurt.
5 Serve straightway, with the vegetables.

serving suggestions
This makes a great accompaniment to lamb chops or other grilled meat, or poultry.

storage
Tzatziki can be stored in the fridge for up to 24 hours but is not suitable for freezing.

allergens
Milk (yogurt).

little bites

moroccan hummus with flatbread

This simple dip if eaten with wholemeal pitta bread, will account for a quarter of your daily requirements of iron and a third of zinc.

serves 4
preparation time 5 minutes
cooking time 0 minutes

400 g can chickpeas in water, drained
1 heaped tbsp tahini paste
juice of 1 lime or ½ lemon
1 clove garlic
1 tsp harissa paste or Moroccan spice paste (ras el hanout)
1–2 tbsp olive oil
approx 50 ml water
wholemeal pitta or breadsticks

1 Place all the ingredients in a food processor or blender and blend until smooth, adding sufficient water to make a smooth paste-like consistency.
2 Chill for at least 30 minutes before serving.

serving suggestions
Eat with and strips of peppers, carrots, cucumber and celery.

storage
The hummus can be stored in the fridge for up to 48 hours but is not suitable for freezing.

allergens
Sesame; pitta bread contain wheat (gluten).

tabbouleh with pine nuts

This great little dish is a surprising source of iron and zinc as well as vitamin E – all of which your baby needs to grow and develop.

serves 3
preparation time 10 minutes
cooking time 15 minutes

120 g mixed quinoa and bulgur wheat, or 60 g of each
2 medium tomatoes, seeds removed, diced
7-cm cucumber (approx 100 g), cut into small dice
½ avocado, diced, tossed in 1 tsp lime juice
1 tbsp mint, chopped
1 tbsp parsley, chopped
black pepper, to taste
50 g pine nuts, toasted

1 Cook the quinoa and bulgur wheat according to the packet instructions.
2 Drain and allow to cool slightly.
3 Mix in the tomatoes, cucumber, avocado and herbs and grind over some black pepper.
4 Serve, sprinkled with the pine nuts.

serving suggestions
Eat as an accompaniment to grilled meat or poultry or alongside the Mediterranean Vegetable Parcels, *page 61.*

storage
Tabbouleh is best served freshly made to preserve its vitamin content but it can be stored in the fridge for up to 24 hours.

allergens
Wheat (gluten), pine nuts.

sardine and pepper strudels

This very tasty simple recipe packs in a lot of baby-friendly nutrients per mouthful. As well as calcium, you'll be enjoying omega 3 fatty acids, vitamins B_{12} and D, all of which are baby body-building essentials. If you're not usually a sardine fan, just try this, and you may be surprised just how good it tastes!

serves 2
preparation time 15 minutes
cooking time 15 minutes

2 sheets filo pastry (about 100 g)
oil mister
4 canned sardines in oil, drained
1 tbsp lemon juice
½ red bell pepper, finely sliced
2 tsp fresh coriander, chopped
grated zest of ½ lemon
black pepper, to taste

1 Preheat the oven to 200°C, 180°C for fan oven or gas mark 6.
2 Place one sheet of filo pastry on a clean, dry work surface or chopping board, and spray with a little oil.
3 Place 2 of the sardines on the pastry and top with half of the lemon juice, sliced pepper, coriander and lemon zest. Season with a little black pepper.
4 Roll up the pastry, tucking the ends under, and place on a lightly-oiled baking sheet or one lined with baking parchment. Repeat steps 2 through 4 to make the second parcel. Spray parcels with some more oil, and bake for 15 minutes or until golden.

serving suggestions
Garnish with sliced lemon and eat with a salad of mixed leaves and sliced fresh tomatoes.

storage
The strudel can be kept in an airtight container in the fridge for up to 24 hours but is not suitable for freezing. Reheat until piping hot.

allergens
Wheat (gluten), fish.

VARIATION
If you prefer, use sardines in tomato sauce, or canned mackerel; canned tuna isn't such a nutritious substitute.

home-made fish goujons
with piquant avocado dip

Use your favourite sustainable white fish such as hake, cod, haddock, basa or pollock to make these goujons. Serving them with the piquant dip will meet more than 50 per cent of your pregnancy requirement for vitamin B_{12}, and provides more than one quarter of the calcium and magnesium your baby needs for her bones and teeth.

serves 2–3
preparation time 15 minutes
cooking time 15 minutes

2 hake fillets or other white fish (approx 240 g)
2 slices wholegrain bread made into breadcrumbs or
*   50–60 g ready-made breadcrumbs*
zest of ½ lime, finely grated
black pepper
1 small egg, beaten

for the piquant avocado dip
½ avocado, cut into small cubes
zest of ½ lime, finely grated
1 tsp lime juice
20 g cornichons (small gherkins), finely chopped
175 g Greek yogurt
black pepper

1 Preheat the oven to 200°C, 180°C for fan oven or gas mark 6.
2 Cut the fish fillet into strips around 2 cm wide.
3 Mix the breadcrumbs with the lime zest and black pepper and spoon on to a plate.
4 Line a baking sheet with baking parchment or non-stick liner.
5 Pour the well-beaten egg into a shallow dish.
6 Carefully dip each strip of fish into the egg, and coat well, then transfer to the breadcrumbs. Spoon over the crumbs and press lightly so they adhere. Carefully lift fish on to the baking sheet.
7 Bake the fish for 10–15 minutes or until crispy. Test one piece of fish; it should be easy to break. Set fish aside while you make the dip.
8 Combine the cubes of avocado with the lime zest and juice. Stir in the cornichons and yogurt and season with black pepper.

serving suggestions
Eat the fish hot with the dip *on its own alongside other small plates such as Patatas Bravas, page 60 or Tabbouleh with Pine Nuts, page 64.*

storage
Both goujons and dip are best served straightaway, but the dip can be stored in the fridge for up to 24 hours.

allergens
Wheat (gluten), eggs, fish.

<piquant avocado dip

ratatouille with halloumi and bread

A stew made from peppers, courgette, aubergine, tomatoes and onion, known as ratatouille in France, makes a delicious side dish or accompanied by lightly fried halloumi cheese and pitta bread, can be eaten as a simple lunch or substantial starter that provides essential vitamins A and C, as well as a range of different flavours and textures. If you've never tried halloumi before, be prepared to be enticed by its great taste and versatility in cooking – fried or grilled it shines. It is, however, high in salt, so don't go overboard!

serves 4
preparation time 15 minutes
cooking time 45–50 minutes

for the ratatouille
1 tbsp olive oil
1 medium onion, sliced
2 cloves garlic, crushed
2 peppers of different colours, cut into large dice
1 small aubergine, cut into 2-cm dice
1 medium courgette, cut into 2-cm dice
3 medium tomatoes, quartered
400 g can chopped tomatoes in tomato juice
1 tbsp oregano, chopped

250 g halloumi, sliced
1 tbsp olive oil
4 pitta bread

1 Heat 1 tbsp olive oil in a large ovenproof casserole and fry the onion and garlic for 3–4 minutes.
2 Add the peppers, aubergine and courgette and stir over a medium heat for 5 minutes.
3 Stir in the fresh and canned tomatoes and oregano.
4 Cover and cook over a low heat stirring occasionally, or place in an oven at 180°C, 160°C for fan assisted or gas mark 6 for about 40–45 minutes either method.
6 Meanwhile, heat 1 tbsp olive oil and fry the halloumi until golden on one side, then turn and cook the other side similarly.
7 Lightly toast the pitta bread, and slice into strips.
8 Serve the ratatouille hot with the halloumi and pitta bread strips alongside.

serving suggestions
The ratatouille on its own makes a tasty accompaniment to steak, grilled chicken or fish and will serve 4–6. After cooking, add 1 tbsp chopped parsley and a few basil leaves, torn roughly.

storage
The ratatouille can be stored in the fridge for up to 48 hours though it will lose some of its vitamin C content. It can also be frozen for up to 3 months and reheated until piping hot.

allergens
Wheat (gluten), milk (halloumi).

little bites

bean and salsa wrap

For an easy way to boost your fibre intake tuck some spinach leaves, grated cheese and warmed refried beans into a wrap. This will provide you with half your daily requirements for vitamin A and calcium too.

serves 1
preparation time 5 minutes
cooking time 2 minutes

1 seeded or wholemeal tortilla wrap, warmed
½ small can (215 g) refried beans, warmed
1 tbsp tomato salsa or relish
25 g baby spinach leaves
25 g reduced fat cheddar cheese, grated

1 Spread the warmed beans over the wrap and add the relish.
2 Sprinkle over the cheese and spinach leaves.
3 Roll up the wrap and cut in half.
4 Serve at once.

serving suggestions
Serve with a few cherry tomatoes or a low fat dip and celery crudités.

allergens
Gluten (wheat), milk (cheese). sesame if seeded wraps used.

beef and beet sandwich

You can make a simple highly nutritious sandwich with roast beef which is rich in iron. Teamed here with folate-rich beetroot, horseradish and watercress you'll enjoy a superb sandwich.

serves 1
preparation time 5 minutes
cooking time 0 minutes

1 level tbsp. creamed horseradish
1 level tbsp. greek style yogurt
2 medium slices wholemeal bread
60 g sliced lean beef
40 g sliced cooked beetroot
20 g watercress
olive spread

1 Mix together the horseradish and yogurt and spread over one slice of the bread.
2 Place the beef, beetroot and watercress on top.
3 Spread the remaining slice with olive spread and use to make the sandwich.
4 Serve at once.

serving suggestions
Serve with a few carrot sticks, and a glass of orange juice.

storage
The sandwich will keep over night in the fridge if wrapped in film, but is best served straight away.

allergens
Gluten (wheat), milk (yogurt).

sardine and cheese toastie

Canned sardines should be a store-cupboard essential in pregnancy as they are so good for you and your baby. This simple sandwich lunch ticks so many of your pregnancy nutrition boxes, containing omega 3 fatty acids, vitamins B12 and D, calcium, iron and zinc. In fact you should make it a weekly lunch!

serves 1
preparation time 5 minutes
cooking time 3-4 minutes

2 canned sardines in oil (approx. 60g), drained
1 tsp lemon juice
2 thick slices bread with added fibre
1 few slices red pepper (around 50g)
1 slice (25 g) reduced fat Cheddar cheese

1 Mash the sardines and lemon juice with a fork and spread over one slice of the bread.
2 Add the sliced pepper and top with the cheese. Add the other piece of bread to make a lid.
3 Place in a sandwich toaster until the cheese has melted and the bread is golden.
4 Serve at once.

serving suggestions
Serve with a handful of salad leaves or a few cherry tomatoes

allergens
Gluten (wheat), fish.

egg, tomato and onion roll

This simple filled egg roll provides your baby with bone building calcium and immune boosting zinc as well as tasting great. Instead of full fat mayonnaise it uses a combination of yogurt and low fat mayonnaise with spring onions and tomatoes, to provide a fresh tang rather than cloying taste. Use granary bread or rolls as they provide more folic acid than other breads (unless they have been fortified)

serves 1
preparation time 5 minutes
cooking time   10 minutes

1 medium free range egg
1 medium tomato (around 85 g)
1 level tbsp low fat natural yogurt
1 level tbsp 'lite' mayonnaise (less than 3% fat)
2 spring onions, chopped
black pepper to taste
1 large granary roll or 2 slices granary bread

1 Hardboil the egg and cool immediately in cold, running water.
2 Skin the tomato, remove the seeds and chop roughly
3 Mix the yogurt and mayonnaise with the spring onion and tomato and season with black pepper.
4 When the egg is cool enough, peel and chop into the mix and stir well.
5 Halve the roll and spoon the egg mixture over the base. Pop on the top and eat at once.

serving suggestions
Serve with a handful of rocket or watercress.

storage
The sandwich could be refrigerated wrapped in film for 24 hours, but is best served at once. It is not suitable for freezing.

allergens
Contains: gluten (wheat), eggs, milk (yogurt).

>barley and roasted vegetable salad with pumpkin seeds

little bites

70

barley and roasted vegetable salad with pumpkin seeds

This high-fibre salad is an ideal way to use up remaining roasted vegetables, but you can obviously start from scratch if you prefer. Offset any vitamin losses from using leftovers, by adding in fresh ingredients, in this case parsley and pomegranate seeds. The barley and pumpkin seeds also provide nearly half your day's requirement for blood and bone building iron.

serves 1
preparation time 10 minutes
cooking time 5 minutes

25 g pumpkin seeds
½ recipe of Herbed Barley, page 137
½ recipe of Roast Beet and Butternut Squash, page 135
1 dessertspoon freshly chopped parsley
25 g pomegranate seeds

1 Toast the pumpkin seeds either in a dry frying pan on the hob or in a preheated oven at 200°C, 180°C for fan assisted or gas mark 6 until just lightly browned and crisp. Cool.
2 Meanwhile combine the barley and roasted vegetables, and stir in the parsley.
3 Sprinkle over the pomegranate and pumpkin seeds and serve.

serving suggestions
Accompany with a glass of unsweetened juice.

allergens
Gluten (barley).

> **COOK'S TIP**
> *When pomegranates are out of season, use a few little ripe tomatoes, or a quarter of a chopped red pepper instead.*

little bites

71

cos, chicken and croûtons

A lighter version than the usual fat-laden chicken Caesar salad, this dish provides essential B vitamins to help release energy, and vitamin C for your baby's many developing cells.

serves 1
preparation time 5 minutes
cooking time 15 minutes

1 thick slice seeded bread
olive oil or other vegetable oil spray
60 g cos lettuce, shredded
50 g (¼ medium) red pepper, diced
2 spring onions, cut into 1 cm slices
50 g cooked chicken breast pieces
1 tbsp French dressing

1 Preheat the oven to 200°C, 180°C for fan oven or gas mark 6.
2 Cut the bread into rough cubes and spray with the oil. Bake until crispy, about 10-15 minutes.
3 Meanwhile prepare the other salad ingredients and place in a serving bowl.
4 When the croutons are ready, add to the salad and stir in the French dressing and serve at once.

serving suggestions
This is a complete dish, but if you are still hungry, add some more seeded bread.

allergens
Gluten (wheat), may contain sesame seeds in bread.

quinoa, feta and spinach salad

This simple salad ticks many of the pregnancy nutrition essentials boxes as well as tasting great! It supplies iron (interestingly mostly from the quinoa rather than the spinach), calcium, zinc, as well as vitamins A, B3 and C. So enjoy it knowing you and your baby are benefitting.

serves 2
preparation time 5 minutes
cooking time 20 minutes

120 g quinoa
60 g baby spinach leaves
50 g sundried tomatoes in oil, drained and chopped
100 g feta cheese, cut into cubes
1 small courgette, washed and diced
black pepper

1 Cook the quinoa according to the packet instructions. Allow to cool.
2 Meanwhile wash and spin dry the spinach leaves and place in two salad bowls.
3 When the quinoa is cooked and still warm stir in the tomatoes, feta and courgette and season with black pepper.
4 Spoon on top of the spinach leaves and serve at once.

serving suggestions
Serve with a glass of unsweetened citrus juice to aid iron absorption.

storage
Once the salad has been made it is not suitable for storage, but the cooked quinoa may be refrigerated for up to 48 hours or frozen for 2 months.

allergens
Milk (cheese).

watercress and salmon salad

Full of immune-boosting vitamin A, watercress is a great partner for salmon which supplies essential omega 3 fatty acids and vitamin D. For simplicity choose poached salmon from the deli or lightly smoked chunky slices, opting for the lowest in salt. Finish with a simple drizzle of balsamic glaze.

serves 1
preparation time 5 minutes
cooking time 0 minutes

30 g watercress, washed and drained
70 g poached salmon
4 mozzarella 'cherries' (about 40 g) , halved
6–8 cherry tomatoes, halved
balsamic glaze

1 Break the watercress into small florets and place in the serving dish.
2 Flake the salmon on top, and add the tomatoes and mozzarella.
3 Drizzle over some balsamic glaze and serve at once.

serving suggestions
Accompany with bread or new potatoes, or the Hot Potato Salad, *page 138.*

allergens
Fish.

asparagus risotto

A vegetarian risotto made with folate-rich asparagus, which will slip down easily on days when you are not feeling like eating rich food. Parmesan cheese is safe to eat in pregnancy even if it is unpasteurised.

serves 2
preparation time 5 minutes
cooking time 20–25 minutes

1 medium onion, finely chopped
2 tbsp olive oil
150 g short grain or risotto rice
25 ml of white vermouth or dry white wine (optional)
400 ml reduced salt vegetable stock
200 g fine asparagus, trimmed and cut into ½ cm pieces
1 tbsp finely chopped parsley
30 g finely grated Parmesan cheese
juice of 1 lemon
black pepper, to taste

1 Fry the onion in the oil in a non-stick saucepan for 3-4 minutes to soften but don't brown.
2 Add the rice and stir well, then pour in the vermouth or dry white wine, if used, and cook over medium heat.
3 When the vermouth or wine has bubbled off, stir in 100ml of the vegetable stock and allow it to be absorbed.
4 Then stir in another 100 ml of stock and allow it to be absorbed. Continue adding stock and waiting for it to be absorbed until all the stock is used.
5 When there is no stock left, stir in the asparagus, cover and cook over medium heat for 5 minutes.
6 The risotto should now be ready, with soft rice and tender asparagus. Remove from the heat and stir in the parsley, Parmesan and lemon juice. Check for seasoning, adding black pepper to taste.

serving suggestions
Accompany with additional Parmesan or Cheddar cheese, and a green salad.

allergens
Milk (Parmesan).

Chinese beef and noodles

Rich in iron and zinc, beef is a great food for you and your baby. You can use any frying steak for this recipe, and a 160-gram rump steak makes two generous portions along with mushrooms and noodles.

serves 2
preparation time 10 minutes
cooking time 20 minutes

1 tbsp vegetable oil
1 small onion, sliced
2 cloves garlic, crushed
1-cm piece ginger, grated
160 g chestnut mushrooms, sliced
1 tbsp flour
1 tsp Chinese five spice
160 g frying steak, cut into 1-cm wide strips
250 ml beef stock
1 tbsp soy sauce
300 g (2 sachets) medium, straight-to-wok noodles
1 head (around 160 g) pak choi, cut in half
   lengthwise

1 Heat the oil in a medium-sized, non-stick. lidded sauté pan and fry the onion, garlic and ginger for 2–3 minutes.
2 Stir in the mushrooms, and fry for another 2-3 minutes, until they start to soften.
3 Meanwhile place the flour, spice and strips of steak in a clean food bag and shake until the steak is coated with the flour.
4 Stir the seasoned steak into the mushroom-and-onion mix and cook for 2-3 minutes over a medium heat, turning frequently, until the steak is just brown.
5 Pour the stock and soy sauce over the mixture, stir, cover and simmer gently until the onions and mushrooms are just tender. There should still be lots of fairly runny sauce but add a little water if the sauce is overly thick.
6 Now stir in the noodles, and place the pak choi on top. Cover and continue cooking over a low heat for 4-5 minutes or until the pak choi is wilted and just tender. Serve at once in two warmed bowls.

storage
The complete dish is not suitable for storage, but you can cook up to the end of step 5 and refrigerate the mixture for 2 days or freeze it for up to 3 months. If freezing, defrost in the fridge overnight, then complete the recipe from step 6.

allergens
Gluten (wheat), soya.

one-pot dishes

75

chorizo and black eyed beans with giant cous cous

Black eye beans are peculiarly rich in folate (folic acid), and are readily available in cans in the supermarket, or you can buy dried beans to soak and boil. Combined with chorizo and giant cous cous with a little spinach thrown in at the last minute, gives you a highly nutritious meal for two on the table in less than 30 minutes.

serves 2
preparation time 5–10 minutes
cooking time 15 minutes

100 g chorizo sausage, skin removed and cubed
½ onion, finely chopped
1 stick celery, finely sliced
2 cloves garlic, crushed
1 tsp ground cumin
1 tsp ground coriander
240 g cooked black eye beans or 400 g can black
 beans in water, drained and rinsed
60 g giant wholewheat cous cous
250 ml water
100 g spinach leaves, rinsed

1 Heat the chorizo cubes in a medium heavy-bottomed saucepan (a cast iron casserole pan is ideal) over medium heat to release some of the fat, then stir in the onion, celery and garlic. Cook gently until the onion is starting to soften, reducing the heat slightly if the onion starts to brown too much.
2 Stir in the spices, then add the beans, cous cous and water and bring to the boil.
3 Stir, cover and simmer gently for 10 minutes, stirring occasionally.
4 Meanwhile place the spinach in a colander and wilt by pouring boiling water over it.
5 When the cous cous is just tender, stir in the spinach and heat for a couple more minutes. Serve at once in two warmed bowls.

serving suggestions
Pour over a little lemon juice.

storage
This may be stored in the fridge for 24 hours, and reheated until piping hot. It is not suitable for freezing.

allergens
Gluten (cous cous), celery, chorizo may contain wheat, milk or sulphites.

one-pot dishes

jambalaya

This Creole dish is rich in protein and is a great source of B vitamins especially B_{12}, niacin (B_3) and thiamine (B_1). It makes a quick nutritious supper, which minimises washing up and maximises taste. Cajun spices are often salted, and the chorizo and prawns are salty too, so don't be tempted to add any more.

serves 2
preparation time 10 minutes
cooking time 20–25 minutes

70 g chorizo bought as a piece and cubed
1 small onion, roughly chopped
100 g pork tenderloin, cut into small pieces
½ small green or red pepper, roughly chopped
150 g rice, rinsed
1 tsp Cajun spice
small can (200 g) chopped tomatoes in juice
300 ml water
100 g cooked prawns
1 tbsp chopped parsley

1 Heat the chorizo in a non-stick lidded sauté pan over a low heat to allow the fat to be released. Then add the onion and cook for 5 minutes until the onion softens, stirring occasionally.
2 Add the pork and peppers and turn up the heat a little. Cook for 5 minutes stirring frequently.
3 Add the rice, Cajun spice, tomatoes and water and bring to the boil. Cover and reduce the heat and allow to cook until the rice is almost tender, about 12–15 minutes. Stir occasionally, checking to see if more water is needed and add more water, if required.
4 When the rice is just tender stir in the cooked prawns and heat through.
5 Spoon into two bowls and sprinkle with the parsley.

serving suggestions
Accompany with some petit pois, which can be added to the pan along with the prawns during the last few minutes of cooking.

storage
The jambalaya will keep for 24 hours in the fridge but will be less rich in vitamins than when freshly cooked.

allergens
Shellfish. chorizo may contain milk, wheat and sulphites.

pork and roasted vegetable tray bake

This simple dish centres around pork mince made into balls, which are nestled into vegetables and roasted in a hot oven for a delicious supper. Pork is rich in thiamine (vitamin B_1), which helps to release energy from food, so this is a great meal if you are feeling a little lethargic.

serves 2
preparation time 10 minutes
cooking time 50–60 minutes

200 g waxy potatoes, such as Charlotte or Estima,
  cut into wedges
200 g butternut squash, cubed
½ red pepper, cut into wide strips
1 small red onion, cut into wedges
90 g cherry tomatoes
2 tbsp olive oil
200 g lean pork mince
1 slice white bread, ripped into several pieces
1 clove garlic
few sage leaves or 1 tsp dried sage
1–2 tsp Cajun seasoning (optional) or black pepper

1 Preheat the oven to 200°C, 180°C for fan oven or gas mark 6
2 To evenly coat the vegetables with oil, place all the vegetables in a clean food bag and tip in the olive oil. Shake to coat then tip vegetables into a 25 x 25cm roasting pan.
3 Place the pork, bread, garlic and sage in a blender or food processor and process until mixed together. Shape into 8 evenly sized balls, and tuck amongst the vegetables.
4 If you like Cajun seasoning, sprinkle over all the ingredients. Alternatively use a little black pepper.
5 Place the tray in the oven and cook until golden brown. After 20–25 minutes, remove the pan from the oven and turn over the vegetables and pork balls. Replace and continue cooking for the suggested time or until the pork balls and potatoes are golden.
6 Serve straight away.

serving suggestions
Accompany with a ready-made salsa or a low-fat soured cream dip if you have used Cajun seasoning or with Apple, Sage and Walnut Sauce, *page 104.*

allergens
Gluten (bread).

sausage and orzo hotpot

Quick, filling and full of vital iron and vitamin C, this simple hotpot uses sausages of your choice, and cooks in less than half a hour.

serves 2
preparation time 5 minutes
cooking time 20–25 minutes

3–4 premium sausages of your choice (about 200g)
1 medium onion, finely chopped
1 tbsp vegetable oil
400 g can chopped tomatoes in juice
130 g orzo
200 ml chicken stock
1 tsp oregano
100 g baby spinach leaves

1 Remove the skin from the sausage, and make each into 3 balls.
2 Add the oil to a non-stick lidded sauté pan and fry the sausage balls for 4–5 minutes, stirring occasionally until they are brown all over. Remove from the pan and drain on kitchen paper.
3 Add the onion to the pan and fry in the cooking juices for 5 minutes or until lightly browned.
4 Return the sausage balls to the pan, and stir in the orzo, tomatoes, stock and oregano.
5 Cover and bring to simmering point, then cook for 10 minutes stirring occasionally until the orzo has absorbed much of the liquid and is nearly tender. Add more stock or water if all the liquid is used and the orzo needs more cooking.
6 When the orzo is tender, stir in the spinach, re-cover and cook for 2 more minutes or until the spinach has just wilted. Serve at once.

serving suggestions
Accompany with a crisp green salad.

storage
The hotpot is best served at once, but can be kept in an airtight container in the fridge for 24 hours. Reheat until piping hot in a microwave oven. Not suitable for freezing.

allergens
Gluten (pasta, possibly sausages).

one-pot dishes

pot roasted chicken

This meal is a great one to do for visitors as all the preparation is at the beginning and once it is in the oven you can sit back and relax. If you prefer not to cook the asparagus at the end, simply add to the casserole around 30 minutes before you expect it to be ready.

serves 4–5
preparation time 15 minutes
cooking time 1½ hours

1 tbsp vegetable oil
1 whole medium free range chicken
4 medium (about 400 g) trimmed leeks, cut into 5-cm lengths
350 g new potatoes, scrubbed and halved, if large
1 large (about 450 g) sweet potato, peeled and cut into large cubes
800 ml reduced salt chicken stock
few parsley stalks
2 bayleaves
400 g asparagus, 1 cm cut off the stalks

VARIATION

The chicken carcass can be boiled to make excellent stock for soups – just cover with water, add an onion, carrot, peppercorns and a bayleaf or two, and simmer for 2-3 hours. Strain and chill or freeze.

1 Preheat the oven to 200°C, 180°C for fan oven or gas mark 6.
2 Fry the whole chicken in a large casserole or pan for 10 minutes until lightly brown all over.
3 Place in an ovenproof dish large enough to hold the chicken and the vegetables. Add the leeks, potatoes and sweet potato.
4 Pour in the stock and add a few parsley stalks. Cover and bake for one and a half hours, or until the chicken is cooked through and the juices run clear when tested with a sharp knife.
5 Lift out the chicken and place on a carving dish, cover with foil and allow to rest for about 15 minutes. Meanwhile, keep the vegetables warm, and warm some serving dishes.
6 Lightly steam the asparagus using a basket steamer or purpose-made asparagus steamer.
7 When ready to serve, carve the chicken, remove the parsley stalks and accompany with the vegetables and gravy.

storage
The chicken can be removed from the bone and either frozen or kept refrigerated for 2 days. The vegetables can also be refrigerated for 2 days, but will be less rich in nutrients than when served freshly.

STEAMING ASPARAGUS

If you don't have a steamer, place your spears upright into a deep saucepan containing 10cm simmering water, and wedge them into place using balls of aluminium foil. Cover with a dome of foil and simmer for 5–7 minutes, or until tender.

Italian chicken gnocchi

Gnocchi are little Italian dumplings, so are ideal for cooking on top of a simple chicken stew. This comforting one-pot meal contains iron and folate, making it ideal in early pregnancy when your needs for folic acid are very high.

serves 2
preparation time 10 minutes
cooking time 20 minutes

1 tbsp olive oil
1 small onion, finely chopped
1 small fennel bulb, trimmed and roughly chopped
150 g boneless chicken thighs, skinned and cubed
2 cloves garlic, crushed
430 g jar passata rustica
1 tbsp chopped herbs such as basil or oregano
150 g small spinach leaves, washed
350 g ready-made gnocchi

1 Heat the oil in a non-stick sauté pan, and fry the onion and fennel for 4-5 minutes to soften slightly.
2 Stir in the chicken and garlic and continue to fry until the chicken is just starting to brown.
3 Pour in the passata and bring to simmering point. Then cover and heat gently for 10 minutes.
4 Meanwhile, put the spinach in a colander and pour boiling water over it to wilt it. You may need to heat 2 kettles. Using a spatula, press down on the spinach to remove any excess water.
5 Stir the herbs and wilted spinach into the pan, and pop the gnocchi on top. If the mixture looks a little dry, stir in a couple tablespoons of water.
6 Re-cover and continue to cook for 3-4 minutes until the gnocchi are hot through. Serve at once.

serving suggestions
You may want to sprinkle Parmesan cheese on top, or serve with a side salad.

storage
The cooked dish up to the end of step 3 can be refrigerated for up to 24 hours, or frozen. Simply reheat the chicken and sauce, and continue from step 4.

allergens
Gluten (wheat)

paella

Paella has to be a classic one-pot dish, and there are as many variations as there are cooks. Make this one to share with friends for a simple supper, which is has nutritional benefits for you and the baby too. Using red peppers, and fresh tomatoes alongside the peas provides plenty of vitamin C as well as zinc from the meat and fish, which will keep your immune system topped up.

serves 4
preparation time 15 minutes
cooking time time 25–30 minutes

2 tbsp olive oil
I medium onion, finely chopped
250 g chicken breast fillet or thigh, finely cubed
2 cloves garlic, crushed
2 large tomatoes,
1 large red pepper, sliced
½ tsp saffron threads, ground (optional)
1 tsp paprika
2 bay leaves
250 g paella or short grain rice
450 ml low salt chicken stock, hot
100 g prawns of your choice, but if frozen, thawed
100 g squid, sliced
150 g petit pois

1 Heat the oil in a shallow frying pan or paella pan, and cook the onion for 5 minutes, or until lightly browned and soft.
2 Add the chicken and garlic, and cook over a low heat for 5 minutes.
3 Meanwhile, skin (see page 123) and chop the tomatoes, removing the seeds, and slice the peppers.
4 Add these to the pan along with the saffron (if using), paprika and bay leaves.
5 Stir in the rice and cook for a couple of minutes stirring all the time to prevent sticking, before adding the stock. Stir through once and allow the mixture to bubble, uncovered for around 15 minutes.
6 Finally add the prawns, squid and petit pois and cook until these are cooked through, around 5–10 minutes. Stir in a little more stock or water, if needed.

7 If you are using raw prawns, ensure they are pink throughout before serving. Check for seasoning, remove the bay leaves and serve at once.

serving suggestions
Accompany with a crisp green salad.

allergens
Fish and shellfish.

>Paella

wild rice pilaff with haddock, peas and capers

In this easy-to-cook meal, the fish, which can be any fillet of your choice, is gently steamed over the cooking rice and vegetables, keeping it moist and succulent. Fish is a pregnancy essential, and this recipe provides zinc and vitamins B_3 and B_{12}, as well as fibre.

serves 2
preparation time 5 minutes
cooking time 35–40 minutes

1 tbsp vegetable oil
1 small leek or 4–5 spring onions, finely sliced
140 g brown basmati and wild rice mix
300 ml water or fish stock
1 tbsp capers
3 bayleaves
few strips lemon rind
120 g frozen peas, defrosted
250 g skinless fillet of haddock
juice of ½ lemon

1 Heat the oil in a lidded non-stick sauté pan and gently soften the leek or spring onion for a few minutes without browning.
2 Wash the rice (see below) then stir it into the pan.
3 Pour in the water or stock, and add the capers, bay leaves and lemon rind.
4 Stir well and bring to simmering point. Stir, cover, and allow to cook gently for 20–25 minutes. or until the brown rice is starting to soften. Add a little more water or stock if there is none visible in the pan.
5 Stir in the peas, and place the fish on top of the pilaff. Pour the lemon juice over the fish and re-cover.
6 Cook for another 10 minutes, or until the fish becomes opaque and flakes easily. Serve at once.

serving suggestions
Accompany with a few sliced ripe tomatoes

allergens
Fish.

WASHING RICE
Most rice, but particularly basmati, benefits from having its excess starch removed by 'washing'. You can either place it in a sieve and run cold water over it or put it in a large bowl, cover with cold water and stir with your fingers. When the rice settles, gently tip the bowl so the water drains away (it will be cloudy). Add more cold water and repeat as necessary untill the water runs clear.

casserole of duck and shallots with peaches

This dish is full of pregnancy essentials, namely zinc and copper, as well as being easy to prepare or cook in advance.

serves 2
preparation time 15 minutes
cooking time 2 hours

1 tbsp vegetable oil
130 g shallots or one medium onion, halved and sliced
2 large duck legs (approx 450g including bone)
2 peaches or nectarines, quartered and stoned
5 cardamon pods, roughly crushed (optional) or a pinch of ground cloves
200 ml water
black pepper to taste

VARIATION
Duck legs are now widely available in supermarkets but if you can't find any, substitute with chicken thighs, and cut down the cooking time by around half an hour.

1 Preheat the oven to 170°C, 150°C for fan oven or gas mark 3.
2 Wash the duck legs and pat dry with kitchen paper.
3 Heat the oil in a non-stick pan and gently fry the shallots until lightly browned, stirring occasionally.
4 Add the duck, fruit, spice and water, cover and place in the oven for approximately 2 hours, or until the duck is really tender.
5 Season with pepper and serve at once.

serving suggestions
Eat with wholegrain rice and steamed broccoli or spinach.

storage
The cooked dish can be kept in an airtight container and refrigerated for up to 2 days. Alternatively it can be frozen for up to 3 months. Defrost overnight in a fridge before reheating until piping hot throughout.

chicken with pine nuts and prunes

Much derided but delicious and a great help to the pregnancy gut, prunes are a good source of iron as well as providing soluble fibre and potassium. This simple casserole with vitamin E-rich pine nuts is sweet and delicious, and can be frozen for use another time. The wine will, of course, be rendered non alcoholic by the time you serve it, so is safe to add.

serves 4
preparation time 10 minutes
cooking time 40-45 minutes

1 tbsp vegetable oil
500 g skinless, chicken thighs
1 medium onion, peeled and sliced lengthwise
250 g ready-to-eat prunes
50 g pine nuts
100 ml dry white wine
2 tbsp chopped parsley
black pepper, to taste

1 Heat the oil in a large, lidded non-stick frying pan and brown the chicken thighs over a medium heat, turning the pieces occasionally.
2 Stir in the onion, lower the heat and cover the pan. Continue to cook for 10 minutes.
3 Add the prunes, pine nuts and wine and cook gently for another 10-15 minutes, or until the chicken is cooked through. Pierce the flesh with a sharp knife and look for clear, not pink, juices.
4 Stir in the parsley, check the seasoning and serve at once.

serving suggestions
Eat with cous cous, Almond Rice (page 136), and a green vegetable such as mangetout, kale or spinach.

storage
The cooked dish is may be kept in an airtight container and refrigerated for up to 2 days. Alternatively, it can be frozen for up to 2 months, defrosting in the fridge overnight and reheating until piping hot.

allergens
Pine nuts (not true nuts but some people are allergic to them).

main dishes poultry

85

chocolate and chilli chicken

If you are craving chocolate in pregnancy but want to stave off the urge to demolish a whole bar, try this Mexican-inspired recipe. You can make it in under half an hour – not as quick as unwrapping a chocolate bar – but much more nutritious!

serves 3
preparation time 5 minutes
cooking time 20-25 minutes

1 tbsp olive oil
1 small red onion, finely chopped
300 g skinless, boneless chicken thighs, each cut
   into 2 or 3 pieces
75 g raisins
1 fresh red chilli, finely chopped, optional
1 tbsp cocoa powder
1 tbsp cornflour
pinch cinnamon
1 heaped tbsp tomato puree
75 ml red wine

1 Heat the oil in a lidded non-stick sauté pan and gently fry the onion and chicken thighs until browned all over, stirring often – about 10 minutes.
2 You should have some cooking liquid remaining, but if not, add a tablespoon of water. Add the raisins, and chilli (if using) and cover with the lid. Cook for another minute or two over a low heat.
3 Meanwhile, mix the cocoa, cornflour, cinammon and tomato puree in a small bowl and gradually stir in the red wine and 125 ml water to make a sauce.

4 Pour the sauce into the cooking liquid, and stir to coat everything.
5 Continue to cook for another few minutes, then check the chicken is cooked through. Test a piece by piercing the flesh with a sharp knife and looking to see if the juices run clear.

serving suggestions
Eat *with a spoonful of yogurt or soured cream accompanied by* Almond Rice, *page 136 or soft corn or wheat tortillas or mashed sweet potato along with seasonal green vegetables.*

storage
This can be stored in an airtight container and refrigerated for up to 2 days. It can also be frozen for up to 3 months, and reheated until piping hot. If frozen, the sauce may separate out a little on defrosting. If this happens, pour off the sauce, and mix with a teaspoon of cornflour. Then heat in a saucepan before mixing back in with the other ingredients and reheating the whole dish.

allergens
Milk (yogurt).

CHILLI HEAT
The volatile oil, capsaicin, while present in the whole pepper is concentrated in the seeds and pith. If you don't want your dish overly spicy, remove them with rubber glove covered fingers or use a small knife. If you don't wear rubber gloves, make sure you wash your hands afterwards.

duck and oriental mushroom stir-fry

Duck breast fillets are widely available in supermarkets and make cooking a nutritious meal simple and quick. The combination of the duck and shitake mushrooms provides more than a quarter of your requirements for iron, with lots of vitamins B$_{12}$ and C.

serves 2
preparation time 10 minutes
cooking time 10 minutes

1 tbsp vegetable oil
225 g duck breast fillets, cut into 3–4 cm slices
150 g shitake mushrooms, halved if large
2 spring onions, cut into 1-cm pieces
½ yellow pepper, sliced
1 small red chilli (optional), finely chopped
100 g fresh beansprouts
1 tsp grated ginger root
1 clove garlic crushed
20 ml mirin rice wine or sweet sherry
20 ml ketjap manis or light soy sauce

1 In a non-stick wok, heat the oil until hot and stir fry the duck for 4-5 minutes stirring all the time.
2 Add the mushrooms, onions and pepper and cook for a further minute or two
3 Add the chilli, beansprouts, garlic and ginger, and stir-fry for two minutes.
4 Remove a piece of duck breast and cut in half to check it is cooked through — the juices should be clear, and the meat pale brown not pink.
5 If the duck is cooked, remove the wok from the heat and stir in the mirin and ketjap manis. If not, continue to fry a little longer before adding the wine and sauce.

serving suggestions
Divide the duck between 2 bowls and eat with plain noodles or coconut rice.

allergens
Soya.

duck with cherry sauce and leek mash

This way of cooking duck breast is great for a special occasion meal. Although duck is known for its fat content, it is not high in saturates, but the more healthy monounsaturated fat. If you want to cut the fat content, remove the skin after cooking and before eating.

serves 2
preparation time 25 minutes
cooking time 30 minutes

200 g fresh cherries, pitted
150 ml chicken stock
50 g cherry jam
1 tbsp sherry or red wine vinegar
2 duck breast fillets (around 150g each)

for the leek mash
1 tbsp olive oil
1 medium leek, washed thoroughly and finely chopped.
375 g old potatoes (Desiree, Maris Piper), peeled
semi skimmed milk to mash
black pepper

1 Simmer the cherries in the chicken stock for 10-15 minutes until tender. Then stir the cherry jam into the sauce along with the vinegar and heat until just bubbling. Remove from heat and allow to cool a little.

2 Meanwhile sweat the leeks in the olive oil over a low heat for 10 to 15 minutes. Do not brown.
3 Boil the potatoes until tender.
4 Place the duck breasts skin side down in a frying pan over a medium to high heat and allow to brown. When the skin is crispy, turn over and cook the other side. Cook thoroughly until the juices run clear when the flesh is pierced by a sharp knife.
5 Drain and mash the potatoes with the milk and stir in the cooked leeks, season with black pepper.

serving suggestions
Spoon the leek mash onto warmed plates and top with the duck breast. Serve with the cherry sauce and accompany with spinach, broccoli or cauliflower.

storage
The sauce and mashed potato can be frozen separately for up to 2 months, and reheated until piping hot. Alternatively the sauce may be refrigerated for 48 hours.

allergens
Milk.

PITTING CHERRIES
A mechanical pitter makes it easy to remove the pits while retaining precious juices and the shape of the fruit.

mozzarella turkey with fig and ginger 'jam'

Thin turkey escalopes or breast slices are quickly pan fried or grilled and topped with a slice of mozzarella for added calcium and taste. When fresh figs are in season, this delicious jam is a great partner it or other turkey or chicken recipes. You'll have enough for four servings so freeze some for when fresh figs are hard to come by.

serves 1
preparation time 10 minutes
cooking time 20 minutes

for the 'jam'
1 tbsp vegetable oil
1 small red onion, finely chopped
2 tsp grated ginger root
4 medium figs, washed, stalk removed and cut into 8 pieces
80 ml water
2 tsp balsamic vinegar

for the turkey
2 turkey escalopes or breast slices (approx. 100 g)
45 g slice of mozzarella
basil leaves, optional

1 To make the jam, heat the oil in a non-stick saucepan and fry the onion gently until soft.
2 Stir in the ginger and figs and cook for a minute or two over a medium heat before stirring in the water and vinegar.
3 Cover and allow the ingredients to simmer gently for 10-15 minutes, stirring occasionally until the mixture is thick and pulpy. Set aside whilst you prepare the turkey.
4 Preheat a grill or griddle pan and lightly spray the turkey with oil.
5 Cook the turkey for 3-4 minutes each side until it is cooked through, then top with a couple of basil leaves, if used, and the mozzarella.
6 Pop under the grill for another couple of minutes, or until the cheese is softened.

serving suggestions
Accompany with one quarter of the fig jam and with new or mashed potatoes, and a seasonal green vegetable.

storage
The turkey is not suitable for storage, but the sauce may be kept in an airtight container and refrigerated for up to 2 days. Alternatively, the sauce may be frozen separately and should be piping hot when reheated.

allergens
Milk (mozzarella).

mushroom stuffed chicken
with puy lentils

Wonderfully rich in minerals, this stylish dish freezes well and looks impressive if you have people over. If you can't be bothered to make parcels, you can add all the stuffing ingredients to the pan and leave out the ham.

serves 4
preparation time 15 minutes
cooking time 1-1¼ hours

1 tbsp olive oil
1 small onion, finely chopped
100 g mushrooms, finely chopped
fine string
4 pieces of Parma or Serrano ham
4 large, boned and skinned chicken thighs
4 large sprigs tarragon
Black pepper
150g puy lentils
3 sticks celery chopped into 2-cm lengths
400 ml dilute chicken stock
2-3 sprigs tarragon or 1 tsp dried

1 Preheat the oven to 180°C, 160°C for fan oven or gas mark 5.
2 Heat the oil in a saucepan and gently fry the onion and mushroom until soft. Allow to cool.
3 Cut 4 lengths of string around 40 cm each.
4 Place a slice of ham on a clean chopping board Then, on top of the ham and perpendicular to it, add a chicken thigh.
5 Spoon a quarter of the mushroom-and-onion mix on to the centre of the thigh, add a sprig of tarragon and a little black pepper.

6 Wrap the ham around the thigh and, with one length of string, tie it in both directions.
7 Repeat until you have 4 chicken parcels.
8 Place the lentils, celery and remaining tarragon in a large ovenproof casserole and add the parcels. Pour over the stock, cover the casserole and place in the oven.
9 As they cook, the lentils will absorb much of the stock, so check occasionally that there is sufficient liquid, adding more water or stock as necessary.
10 Cook for a hour to an hour and a quarter, or until the chicken juices run clear when pierced with a sharp knife.
11 Remove the strings from the chicken parcels and the sprigs of tarragon from the sauce before serving.

serving suggestions
Eat with kale, carrots and brown rice, or Gratin of Potato, *page 139.*

storage
The cooked dish can be refrigerated in an airtight container for 2 days. Alternatively it can be frozen for up to 3 months, thawed overnight in the fridge and reheated until piping hot.

allergens
Celery.

sesame and coriander chicken with mango salsa

Chicken thighs are a better source of minerals such as zinc and iron than breasts. Vitamin C, of course, helps your body absorb iron and along with energy releasing niacin, and essential vitamin B_{12} as well, this dish provides a gestational nutritional boost. And it also tastes great, too!

serves 2
preparation time 15 minutes
cooking time 15 minutes

4 small or 2 large boned, skinless chicken thighs
1 tbsp olive oil
1 tbsp sesame seeds
1 tbsp coriander seeds, lightly crushed
juice of ½ lime
2 cloves garlic, crushed

mango salsa
½ large mango or 100 g mango cubes,
juice of ½ small lemon or lime
½ small red onion
½ red pepper
1 dsp chopped coriander
1 small chilli pepper (optional), very finely chopped

1 Trim any visible fat from the chicken thighs.
2 Mix together the next 5 ingredients in a bowl large enough to hold the chicken pieces. Add the chicken and stir to coat with the marinade. Cover and refrigerate whilst you prepare the salsa.
3 Cut the mango into 1-cm cubes and place in a serving bowl. Pour over the lemon or lime juice.
4 Finely slice the red onion, and cut the pepper into small pieces or slices and add both to the mango.
5 Stir in the coriander and chilli, if using, and chill until required.
6 Heat a griddle pan or grill and remove the chicken from the fridge.

7 Place the thighs on the hot griddle or grill pan. Cook for 5 minutes on each side, then test for doneness. Insert a knife into the flesh and check to see the juices run clear. If not, cook for a couple minutes longer.

serving suggestions
Accompany with the salsa and some boiled new potatoes or coconut rice.

storage
The chicken thighs can be eaten cold so can be refrigerated for up to 48 hours. The salsa is best within 24 hours. Neither is suitable for freezing.

allergens
Sesame.

main dishes poultry

spinach stuffed chicken breasts with proscuitto

A simple and elegant dish, which is lovely to serve for a dinner party or a special supper for 2. The spinach filling provides essential vitamin A.

serves 2
preparation time 15 minutes
cooking time 35 minutes

2 boneless chicken breasts, skinned
50 g thawed chopped frozen spinach, drained
1 rounded tbsp. reduced fat mascarpone cheese
1 tbsp parsley, chopped
rind of ½ lemon, grated,
pinch of grated nutmeg
2 large or 4 small slices Prosciutto (Parma) ham
cocktail sticks or string
1 dsp olive oil

1 Preheat the oven to 180°C, 160°C for fan oven or gas mark 5.
2 Slice horizontally into each chicken breast to make a pocket.
3 Mix the drained spinach with the mascarpone, parsley, lemon and nutmeg.
4 Spoon half the filling into each pocket.

5 Lay the ham on a piece of greaseproof paper and place the stuffed breast on top. Wrap the Prosciutto around the chicken, using the paper to help position it. Secure with cocktail sticks or string.
6 Heat the oil in a non-stick frying pan and cook the breasts on each side for around 3 minutes, or until just browned.
7 Transfer to an ovenproof dish, cover, and bake for around 30 minutes, or until the juices of the flesh run clear when pierced with a knife.
8 Remove the cocktail sticks or string and slice if you wish.

serving suggestions
Eat with boiled new potatoes or a sweet potato mash, and seasonal greens.

allergens
Milk (mascarpone).

STUFF IT!

Chicken and turkey are extremely versatile and there are many different recipes you can make with a few simple ingredients. Rather than simply grilling or frying a chicken breast or turkey escalope, it's easy to bake the chicken or turkey with a filling that adds nutrients to your diet, and looks and tastes great, too. Meat from free range and organically produced flocks can have a more flavoursome taste, so try to buy locally produced or at least British free-range chicken and turkey, which have accredited welfare schemes.

QUANTITIES
These fillings make sufficient to stuff two chicken or two turkey breasts or excalopes.

mushroom and onion
Fry one roughly chopped small onion with 4–5 chopped chestnut mushrooms in 1 tsp of olive oil. Mix in the grated zest of half a lemon and some black pepper.

sundried tomato and soft cheese
Drain 30 g of sundried tomatoes in oil on some kitchen paper and chop roughly. Stir into 45 g (quarter pot) reduced fat soft cheese along with one clove of crushed garlic and a little black pepper.

marinated artichoke and tarragon
Drain 50 g of marinated artichokes on some kitchen paper, then chop roughly. Mix with the zest of one orange, and a few sprigs of fresh tarragon.

walnut, prune and cinnamon
Chop 50 g of ready-to-eat prunes with 30 g walnut pieces and stir in a pinch of ground cinnamon.

VARIATION
For alternative recipes see Spinach Stuffed Chicken Breasts with Proscuitto and Mushroom, *page 92 and* Mushroom Stuffed Chicken with Puy Lentils, *page 90.*

HOW TO STUFF AND WRAP A CHICKEN OR TURKEY BREAST OR ESCALOPE

1 Once you have made the filling, you need to make a large enough pocket in the breast to hold your filling using a sharp knife. Then add the filling to the pocket. Decide if you want to first wrap the chicken or turkey in bacon or pancetta or ham (Prosciutto and Serrano work well) to add moistness to the poultry, or just secure the filling with cocktail sticks or string.

2 If you are using bacon or ham to wrap, flatten the slice out on a piece of greaseproof paper or lightly oiled foil and lay the stuffed breast or escalope on top. Then wrap the breast or escalope up with it, using the paper or foil to help you. Secure with cocktail sticks or string.

3 Transfer the packet, still in the foil or greaseproof paper, to a roasting tin or baking sheet and cook in a preheated oven at 190°C, 170°C for fan oven or gas mark 5 for 30 minutes. Then open the foil or peel off the paper and allow the chicken or turkey to brown for 10 minutes or until the juices in the poultry run clear when pierced with a knife.

4 Serve, remembering to remove the cocktail sticks or string.

turkey herb burgers with fruity salsa

Turkey mince is low in fat, and high in vitamin B$_3$, or niacin, which helps release energy. Combined with some herbs and served with a roll, fruity salsa and mustardy watercress, you'll be providing great nutrition for your baby as well as having a tasty meal. If you buy a 500g pack of mince, you can use half for this recipe and freeze the rest to use later, or double up on the ingredients and make and freeze the whole batch.

serves 2-3
preparation time 15 minutes
cooking time 20–25 minutes

250 g turkey mince
½ small onion, roughly chopped
2 cloves of garlic
2-3 stalks fresh parsley, or ½ tsp dried
flour
1 tbsp vegetable oil

for the fruity salsa
1 large ripe nectarine or peach, skin and stone
   removed
1 ripe medium tomato, skinned
Juice of one medium orange or 50 ml unsweetened
   juice
1 tsp dark brown sugar, optional

to serve
2–3 wholemeal or multi-seed rolls
olive spread
handful of watercress

1 Place the mince, onion, garlic and parsley in a processor and pulse until just combined.
2 Remove and using a little flour on your hands to prevent sticking, shape into 2–3 burgers, depending on appetite. Chill.
3 Meanwhile, roughly chop the peach or nectarine and tomato and place in a small saucepan.
4 Stir in the orange juice and cook gently until the fruit is tender – around 10–15 minutes, adding more juice if the salsa looks dry.
5 Taste, and add a little sugar if required. Allow to cool.
6 Heat the oil oil in a frying pan and gently fry the burgers for around 5-6 minutes each side until the juices run clear when pierced with a knife. Alternatively brush lightly with oil and grill.
7 Warm the rolls and lightly spread with olive spread. Top with the burgers and watercress and serve with the salsa.

storage
Once cooked, the turkey burgers are not suitable for reheating, but whilst raw they can be wrapped individually in cling film and frozen for up to one month. Defrost in the fridge and cook as above. The sauce can be stored in the fridge for 2-3 days, although it will lose B vitamins and vitamin C when stored and reheated.

allergens
Wheat (gluten).

VARIATION
You can make the salsa using canned peaches in juice. Just reduce the amount of orange juice you use. Other variations would be to add vitamin A rich mango, or some ready-to-eat apricots or a few raisins, and some allspice or ground cloves.

teriyaki turkey with sesame cucumber salad

This Japanese-style dish is high on flavour and low in saturated fat. It makes a great light lunch or you can add some rice to turn it into a more substantial evening meal. Turkey is an unusually good source of niacin (vitamin B_3). Both the marinade and salad dressing contain root ginger, which can be a great help in preventing pregnancy nausea.

serves 2
preparation time 15 minutes
cooking time 10 minutes

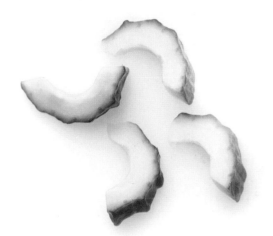

for the teriyaki marinade
30 ml mirin rice wine or sweet sherry
20 ml soya sauce, preferably reduced salt
1 tsp grated lime zest
2 tsp grated ginger root
juice of ½ lime

4 small turkey breast escalopes, (about 60 g each)
*   or 2 larger ones*

for the sesame cucumber salad
½ cucumber
2 cloves garlic, crushed
2 tsp grated ginger root
2 tbsp rapeseed or sunflower oil
pinch of sugar
1–2 tbsp chopped fresh coriander
1 heaped tbsp sesame seeds, toasted

1 Mix together all the marinade ingredients in a bowl and stir in the turkey escalopes so they are coated with the marinade. Cover and refrigerate.
2 Cut the cucumber in half lengthwise and remove the seeds so the cucumber pieces are hollowed out. Cut the lengths into fat slices, each of which will resemble a half moon.
3 Mix together the garlic, ginger, oil and sugar to make a thick dressing and stir in the cucumber pieces.
4 Add the coriander and sesame seeds and chill whilst you cook the turkey.
5 Preheat a griddle or grill. Remove the turkey from the marinade and wipe off any excess – it should just have a little clinging to it.

6 Grill or griddle the turkey on one side for 3-4 minutes before turning to cook the other side a similar time. Depending on the thickness of the turkey, you may need to continue to cook for another minute or so until the flesh is cooked through and the juices run clear.

serving suggestions
Eat with the salad and add rice or udon noodles for a more substantial meal.

storage
The salad is best eaten within 24 hours. The cooked turkey is not suitable for reheating but you could eat any remaining cold within 24 hours with a different salad or sliced in a wrap or tortilla.

allergens
Sesame, soya.

COOK'S TIP
Choosing salt reduced soy sauce can help to keep your salt intake down.

main dishes poultry

95

pork with pineapple

This recipe provides huge amounts of energy releasing B vitamins, even when nutrient losses due to cooking are accounted for. Try griddling the fresh pineapple for a different take on this classic combination.

serves 2
preparation time 15 minutes
cooking time 15 minutes

300 g pork tenderloin, cut into 1.5-cm wide slices
200 ml pineapple juice, ideally fresh
1 clove garlic, crushed (optional)
1 tbsp vegetable oil
1 medium onion, finely chopped
1 large stick celery, washed and sliced
1 medium carrot, peeled and sliced
4 thinly sliced rounds of pineapple

1 Place the pork slices and pineapple juice in a bowl with the garlic, if used. Allow to stand for 10 minutes.
2 Meanwhile heat the oil in a non-stick saucepan and add the onion, celery and carrot. Cover and cook over low heat for 5 minutes until soft but not browned.
3 Drain the pork, saving the juice. Pat the pork dry on some kitchen paper.
4 Add the pineapple juice to the vegetable mixture and simmer until the vegetables are just tender, adding a little water if the mixture is too dry.
5 Heat a griddle and spray with cooking oil. When hot, cook the pineapple slices briefly for 2–3 minutes to achieve a griddled appearance. Put to one side.
6 Re-spray the griddle and cook the sliced pork for a few minutes each side until the juices run clear.
7 Serve the pork with the pineapple and the vegetable sauce poured over.

serving suggestions
Eat with cooked pearl barley or brown rice, and a seasonal green vegetable.

storage
The sauce may be refrigerated or frozen but the pork is best freshly cooked.

allergens
Celery.

FOOD SAFETY
Ensure the pork is properly cooked, checking that the juices run clear when you insert a sharp knife.

Chinese pork with plums

Pork is a good source of thiamin (vitamin B$_1$), which helps release energy from foods so is essential for your baby's overall growth and development as well as keeping you well.

serves 2
preparation time 15 minutes
cooking time 15 minutes

1 tbsp vegetable oil
1 small or half pork tenderloin (250-300 g)
1 medium red onion, finely sliced
3 cloves garlic, chopped
3 cm fresh ginger, peeled and cut into fine
  matchsticks
1 tsp Chinese five-spice powder
8 smallish plums stoned and quartered
1 level tbsp soft brown sugar
100 ml water

1 Heat the oven to 150°C, 130°C for fan oven or gas mark 2.
2 Cut the pork into 1-cm slices and, using a non-stick frying pan, cook in 1 tsp of oil for 5 minutes or until lightly browned, then turn and cook for another few minutes until the juices run clear. Keep warm in a covered dish in the oven.
3 Heat the remaining oil and sauté the onion and garlic for a minute or two.
4 Add the ginger, five-spice powder, plums, sugar and water and allow to simmer gently for 10 minutes or until the plums are softened.
5 Pour the plum sauce over the pork and serve.

serving suggestions
Eat with boiled noodles and stir-fried pak choi or other green vegetable.

storage
The sauce may be refrigerated or frozen but the pork is best freshly cooked.

allergens
Milk (if using yogurt or cream).

Hungarian goulash

Made with smoked paprika and red rather than green peppers, this dish is both high in zinc and vitamin A. It freezes well so is a great one to make for later in pregnancy, or for when your baby has arrived and you may have little time or energy to cook..

serves 4
preparation time 10 minutes
cooking time 1 hour 45 minutes to 2 hours

1 tbsp vegetable oil
1 medium onion, halved and then sliced
3 cloves garlic, crushed
1 tbsp plain flour or cornflour
1 tbsp smoked paprika
500 g lean braising or casserole steak, cut into 2-cm cubes
250 g beef stock
400 g can chopped tomatoes
2 medium red peppers, cut into large pieces

1 Preheat the oven to 160°C, 140°C for fan oven or gas mark 3.
2 Heat the oil in a large ovenproof casserole and fry the onion for 5 minutes, or until lightly browned. Stir in the garlic and fry for another minute or so.
3 Meanwhile place the flour and paprika in a clean plastic foodbag and drop in the meat. Shake to coat with the flour.
4 Tip the floured meat and any remaining seasoned flour, into the casserole and stir briefly.
5 Add the stock, tomatoes and red peppers and bring slowly to simmering point, stirring often.
6 Cover and transfer the casserole to the oven and cook for 1½ hours. Stir, and return to the oven until the meat is really tender — 15 to 30 minutes longer..

serving suggestions
Eat with *Gratin of Potato*, page 139 and a green vegetable.

storage
The goulash may be kept in an airtight container and refrigerated for up to 2 days, or frozen for up to 3 months. Defrost overnight in the fridge and ideally reheat in a microwave oven until piping hot.

allergens
Wheat (gluten) if wheat flour used.

VARIATION
If you like your goulash hot, choose hot smoked paprika or add 1 tsp chilli powder to the flour mixture. You may like to serve soured cream or yogurt with a hotter goulash.

beef in beer

Reputed as helpful for promoting breast-milk production, stout helps tenderise braising steak in this winter-warming casserole. Adding a few carrots provides your baby with lots of vitamin A for her eye development as well as boosting your immune system. Freeze extra portions for when your baby has arrived.

---

serves 4

preparation time 10 minutes

cooking time 1½ - 2 hours

---

2 tbsp vegetable oil

2 medium onions, sliced

1 rounded tbsp flour (wheat or corn)

Pepper, to taste

1 tsp dried thyme or few fresh thyme sprigs

450 g lean braising or stewing beef steak, cut into
   2-3-cm pieces

300g carrots, cut into chunks

350 ml stout or dark ale

1 tbsp Worcestershire sauce or mushroom ketchup

200 g open cap mushrooms, sliced

1 Preheat the oven to 160°C, 140°C for fan oven or gas
   mark 3.

2 Heat the oil in a frying pan and fry the onions until
   just softening, about 5 minutes.

3 Meanwhile place the flour in a clean plastic food bag
   and season with the pepper and thyme.

4 Drop in the pieces of steak and shake to coat with the
   seasoned flour.

5 Transfer the onions to an ovenproof casserole dish, and
   add the meat, and any remaining flour and the carrots.

6 Pour over the stout and stir in the Worcestershire
   sauce.

7 Cover and bake in the oven for one hour.

8 Remove the casserole from the oven and stir in the
   mushrooms, Continue to cook until the beef is very
   tender, about 30 to 60 minutes longer.

serving suggestions
Eat with baked potatoes that have cooked alongside the stew, and boiled or stir-fried cabbage or kale.

storage
The stew can be refrigerated for 2 days or frozen for up to 2 months. Defrost overnight in the fridge and reheat until piping hot.

allergens
Fish (if using Worcestershire sauce), gluten (if wheat flour used). Use cornflour if sensitive to wheat.

COOK'S TIP
Using a good quality, thick non-stick sauté pan with a lid is a great way to reduce the amount of fat you use in cooking.

baked beef and sour cherries

Beef is a marvellous source of B vitamins and minerals and one portion of this recipe boasts more than a day's supply of vitamins B_3 and B_{12}, as well as zinc and iron. It contains sweetened sour cherries which add a piquancy to the taste and vitamin A for your baby. The recipe uses red wine, but you needn't worry about this as it will just impart flavour not alcohol because the alcohol will cook off. Make a batch to enjoy now or freeze for when your baby has arrived and time is short.

serves 4
preparation time 10 minutes
cooking time 2–2½ hours

1 rounded tbsp white flour or cornflour
1 tsp mixed dried herbs, or 1 bouquet garni
500 g lean stewing steak, cut into 2-cm cubes
1 tbsp rapeseed oil
1 large onion, roughly chopped
4 cloves garlic, crushed
150 g dried sour sweetened cherries
200 ml red wine (or replace with water)
100 ml water
pepper and salt, if required

1 Preheat the oven to 160°C, 140°C for fan oven or gas mark 3.
2 Place the flour and mixed herbs in a clean plastic bag and add the meat. Shake the bag to coat the meat with the flour and herbs.
3 Heat the oil in a non-stick saucepan. Gently brown the onions and garlic before transferring them to a large lidded casserole or ovenproof dish.
4 Add the meat and cherries and stir in the wine and water.
5 Cover the casserole or dish and place in the oven for 2 hours, then remove and stir. If the meat is already tender, it is ready to serve, but if it needs longer, return the casserole or dish to the oven for another 20–30 minutes.
6 Check the seasoning and serve.

serving suggestions
Eat with wholegrain rice and steamed broccoli or spinach.

storage
You can freeze this in an airtight container for 2-3 months, or keep in the fridge for 48 hours. Defrost in the fridge overnight and reheat until piping hot.

allergens
Wheat (gluten) if wheat flour used. Use cornflour if sensitive to wheat.

>baked beef and sour cherries

steak and broccoli with noodles

No meal is really faster than a stir-fry, and it is worth treating yourself to a small piece of steak to make this quick and iron-rich dish. If available, try some different mushrooms for a change, using Japanese enoki or buna shimeji for added flavour.

serves 2
preparation time 10 minutes
cooking time 5–10 minutes

4-5 florets broccoli, cut into smaller florets
2 nests or approx 120 g dry noodles
2 tbsp vegetable oil
225 g lean steak, rump or sirloin, cut into fine slices
1 red onion, finely sliced
2-3 cloves garlic, crushed
150 g mushrooms (enoki, buna shimeji or button),
   finely sliced
2 tbsp oyster sauce

1 Steam the broccoli florets for 2–3 minutes to blanch them, then put to one side whilst you cook the noodles according to the packet instructions.
2 Meanwhile, heat the oil in a non-stick wok or large frying pan, and fry the steak for 2-3 minutes then add the onion and garlic.
3 Stir fry the steak, onion and garlic for a minute or two longer then add the mushrooms and blanched broccoli. Continue to fry for a minute or so, or until the mushrooms have just softened.
4 Drain the noodles and stir into the steak mix along with the oyster sauce.
5 Serve at once in warmed dishes.

allergens
Wheat (noodles), soya and shellfish (check the oyster sauce label).

GRILL OR GRIDDLE IT...

There are many cuts of meat or poultry that are quickly cooked by popping under the grill, on a barbeque or hob-top griddle, or simply pan-frying. Here, you will find some basic information on how to cook a variety of cuts, chops and steaks, as well as a host of different marinades, hot and cold sauces and salsas you can serve them with

the basics

Any meat or poultry which is to be cooked quickly by, say, grilling needs to be tender, and a little fat, whether present in the flesh, or lightly brushed on the surface keeps the meat moist. Griddling using a ridged cast iron pan allows any fat to drain off the meat, and provides characteristic stripes.

best cuts to use

Beef steaks — rump, fillet, or sirloin
Lamb loin or leg chops, or leg steaks, noisettes (boned, rolled loin chop)
Pork leg steaks or escalopes, chump or loin chops, fillet or tenderloin, spare ribs
Venison haunch, loin or shoulder 'steaks' from young animals or if supermarket pack recommends grilling
Chicken thigh, drumstick, breast, wing — with skin on — can remove before serving
Turkey breast as steak or escalope — if very lean, brush with oil or marinade first
Ostrich thigh steaks or back fillet slices (medallions)
Duck breast cooked with pierced skin, grilled skin side up, or griddled skin side down

grilling

1 Preheat the grill.
2 Check the thickness of the meat. Put thinner cuts closer to the heat source and thicker cuts further away, so you don't burn the meat before the middle is cooked.
3 Turn and brush the meat/poultry with a little oil or marinade every few minutes during grilling to keep it moist.

griddling

1 Preheat the griddle.
2 Brush the meat with oil and place on the hot griddle. (If the griddle pan is really hot when you start, you may not need to brush the meat with oil, but this may also depend on the fat content of what you are cooking.)
3 Leave the meat/poultry for a few minutes without turning to allow searing, then using tongs turn over.
3 If the meat is thick you may need to turn over again.
4 The timings are similar to the grill, but may be a little less for thinner cuts.
5 Cuts more than 3 cm thick are not suitable for griddling.

pan-frying

Grilling and griddling use less fat than pan-frying, so are a healthier cooking method.
1 Measure 1-2 tbsp of vegetable oil into a non-stick pan and heat until the oil is hot , but not smoking.

Grilling times			
Cut	Rare*	Medium	Well done
Beef — steaks (not fillet)	5-6 mins	8-12 mins	15-18 mins
Beef — fillet steak	3-5 mins	6-7 mins	8-10 mins
Pork chops or steaks		10-14 mins	
Lamb chops or steaks		10-14 mins	
Chicken breast			15-20 mins
Turkey steak			12-15 mins
Duck breast			15-20 mins

* in pregnancy you should not eat any meat which is rare or undercooked.

2 Add the meat/poultry and leave for 2–3 minutes without turning to allow the surface to seal.
3 Allow to cook well on one side before turning with tongs to cook on the reverse.
4 Drain the food on kitchen paper before serving.

marinades

Marinades are a popular way of adding flavour to a fairly bland cut. If you want to make your own, you'll need something to provide acid and an oil to carry flavour. Then you can try an endless range of herbs and spices. Whatever you marinate must go in the fridge to minimize the risk of food poisoning.

Juices, vinegars and wines are acidic and will break down the protein in the meat, which may not so much tenderise as to make the surface of the meat mushy. So to ensure you don't overdo the timing, look at the timing suggestions below.

herb marinade

150 ml wine (red for beef or lamb; white for pork)
50 ml oil (rapeseed has a neutral flavour, but you can use olive oil)
50 ml wine vinegar
2-3 cloves garlic, crushed
2 bayleaves
1 tbsp chopped fresh herbs of your choosing e.g parsley, sage, tarragon, rosemary

1 Place all the ingredients in a lidded jar or container and shake well.
2 Pour over the meat and stir well.
3 Cover and refrigerate for a minimum of one hour, turning occasionally
4 Remove the meat from the marinade and drain on kitchen paper.

chicken marinade

Chicken is quite tender so doesn't need lots of tenderising, but a marinade which adds flavour before cooking is great.

2-3 tbsp olive oil
grated zest of one lime or ½ lemon
black pepper
1 clove garlic, crushed
Any of the following:
1 tbsp grainy mustard; 1 tsp dried herbs or 1 tbsp fresh; 2 tsp grated ginger root; 2 tsp grated lemongrass; 1 tsp chilli flakes.

1 Mix all the ingredients in the container to be used for marinating.
2 Add the chicken pieces and stir well.
3 Cover and refrigerate for 15–30 minutes
4 Remove and cook, wiping off any excess marinade if required.

some great combos

- Griddled venison steak with *Wild Mushroom and Rosemary Sauce*
- Grilled lamb chop with *Blackberry sSauce*
- Grilled pork loin chop with *Apple, Sage and Walnut Sauce*
- Barbequed lamb leg steaks with *Kachumbari*
- Pan-fried turkey escalopes with *Mango Salsa*
- Griddled rump steak with *Fruity Sauce*
- Grilled Chicken drumsticks with *Peanut Satay Sauce*
- Pan-fried chicken breasts with *Tarragon Sauce*
- *Lamb and Pepper Koftas with Tzatziki*

Maximum marinade times			
Chicken	Pork	Lamb	Beef
2 hours	4 hours	8 hours	24 hours

> **COOK'S TIP**
> *Making a cut in the surface of the meat will allow the marinade to penetrate.*

sauces

Sauces provide moisture for grilled or griddled meat as well as adding contrasting or enhancing flavours. They can also be a way of adding vitamins and minerals to your meal, although the quantity consumed is not usually sufficient to provide a significant boost.
The following recipes — both warm and cold sauces — are ideal accompaniments to many different types of meats and poultry.

apple, sage and walnut sauce

Pork chops particularly cry out for apple sauce, and this provides sage for a punch and walnuts for additional texture, healthy oils and vitamin E.

serves 4
preparation time 5 minutes
cooking time 10–15 minutes

1 medium cooking apple, such as Bramley, peeled and cubed
100 ml cloudy unsweetened apple juice
3-4 large sage leaves, finely chopped or 1 tsp dried rubbed sage
35 g walnut pieces, finely chopped

1 Place the apple, juice and sage in a non-stick saucepan and cook over a gentle heat until the apple is tender and has 'fallen'. Add a little more juice if required.
2 Add the walnuts, check the seasoning, adding more sage and black pepper if required.
3 Either cool to use later or serve with grilled meat such as pork at once.

serving suggestions
Use to accompany any grilled or griddled pork or other meat.

blackberry sauce

An easy delicious sauce to accompany grilled or griddled meat. This sauce which will freeze tastes especially good with venison, but would make an ideal accompaniment to duck or a piece of steak. Don't worry about the wine — any alcohol will be boiled off.

serves 4
preparation time 5 minutes
cooking time 15 minutes

100 ml red wine
200 g blackberries
2 cardamom pods, crushed (optional)
50 g red currant jelly

1 Place the wine, blackberries and cardamom in a saucepan and bring to the boil.
2 Allow to boil gently for 10 or so minutes, or until the mixture is halved in volume.
3 Stir in the jelly, and allow to simmer for a minute or two.
4 Either cool to use later or serve with grilled meat at once.

serving suggestions
Use to accompany venison, steak or duck.

tarragon sauce

An aniseed scented sauce is a classic accompaniment to chicken, but this version is lower in fat than the classic recipe. By using a little cornflour to stabilise the sauce, you can swap double cream for reduced fat crème fraiche or soured cream.

serves 4
preparation time 5 minutes
cooking time 15 minutes

1 tbsp vegetable oil
1 small onion or medium shallot, very finely
  chopped
250 ml low salt chicken stock
1 tbsp fresh chopped tarragon
1 tsp cornflour
4 level tbsp half fat crème fraiche

1 Heat the oil in a saucepan and fry the onion until just starting to brown.
2 Add the chicken stock and bring to the boil and allow to boil gently for 10 or so minutes, or until the mixture is halved in volume.
3 Stir in the tarragon allow to simmer for a minute or two.
4 Mix the cornflour with a tablespoon of water and stir into the stock; bring to simmering point.
5 Stir in the crème fraiche over a low heat. Either cool to use later or serve with grilled meat at once.

serving suggestions
Serve with chicken or turkey breast or steaks.

STORAGE
The sauces on these two pages may be kept in an airtight container and refrigerated for up to 2 days. Alternatively the sauce smay be frozen separately but when reheating theymust come to the boil before serving.

peanut satay sauce

Now peanuts are back on the menu for mums to be unless of course you are allergic to them, you can enjoy their creaminess in simple sauces such as this. It is a good companion for marinated kebabs, lamb, chicken or even prawn, and adds small quantities of some key minerals such as iron, zinc and copper.

----

serves 4
preparation time 5 minutes
cooking time 5 minutes

----

2 spring onions, chopped into fine slices
1 small red chilli, finely chopped (optional)
80 g chunky peanut butter
25 g coconut cream
1 tsp soy sauce
1 tsp fish sauce
175 ml water
juice of 1 lime

1 Place all the ingredients except the lime in a saucepan and stirring all the time bring to simmering point.
2 Remove from the heat and stir in the lime juice
3 Serve hot.

serving suggestions
Serve with chicken or lamb kebabs.

storage
The sauce may be kept in an airtight container and refrigerated for 2 days.

allergens
Peanuts, soya.

wild mushroom and rosemary sauce

In the autumn you can you can buy many different types of wild mushrooms — from chanterelle (girolle) to shitake or porcini (cep). Each has different amount of B vitamins and iron, but not usually sufficient in a sauce to get excited about.

----

serves 4
preparation time 5 minutes
cooking time 15 minutes

----

25 g spread high in monounsaturates, e.g. olive spread
200 g mixed mushrooms, e.g. 150 g chestnut and 50 g 'wild'; sliced or if small, left whole
1 level tbsp plain flour
250 ml low salt beef stock
1 tbsp fresh chopped rosemary

1 Heat the spread in a non-stick saucepan and fry the mushrooms for 5-6 minutes until tender.
2 Add the flour and cook for 1—2 minutes, stirring constantly then gradually add the stock and half the rosemary.
3 Bring to the boil and allow to boil gently for 10 or so minutes, or until the mixture is halved in volume.
4 Check for seasoning and add the remaining rosemary.
5 Either cool to use later or serve with grilled meat at once.

serving suggestions
Serve with any grilled or griddled meat or poultry.

storage
The sauce may be kept in an airtight container and refrigerated for up to 2 days. Alternatively the sauce may be frozen separately but when reheating it must come to the boil before serving.

pot roasted lamb shanks

Lamb is a great source of iron and zinc, and this recipe provides more than half your requirement for zinc and a quarter of your need for iron. Slow cooked in the oven, this pot roast will provide two portions for now and two, which can be frozen for another time.

serves 4
preparation time 15 minutes
cooking time 2 hours

2 tbsp vegetable oil
1 large onion, halved and sliced
3 large sticks of celery, cut into 2-cm pieces
3 medium carrots, scrubbed and thickly sliced into chunks
2 medium lamb shanks (around 750 g)
1 tsp dried mixed herbs or 1 bouquet garni
3 bayleaves
400 ml water
50 ml balsamic vinegar
2 level tbsp plain flour

1 Preheat the oven to 170°C, 150°C for fan oven or gas mark 3.
2 Heat the oil in a non-stick pan and add the onion, celery and carrots. Cook over a medium heat for about 5 minutes, or until they brown slightly. Remove the vegetables.
3 Adding a little more oil if necessary to the pan, brown the lamb shanks over a high heat for 2–3 minutes.
4 Place the lamb and vegetables in a lidded ovenproof dish and add the herbs. Pour over 350 ml water and the vinegar, cover and place in the oven for 1½ hours.
5 Remove from the oven. Mix the flour with 50 ml water and stir into the stew to thicken.
6 Re-cover the dish and return to the oven for another 30 minutes, or until the vegetables are tender, the lamb cooked through and the sauce thickened.
7 Remove the bay leaves and ease the meat away from the bone with a fork before serving.

serving suggestions
Eat with Leek Mash, page 88 and a vitamin C-rich green vegetable such as kale or broccoli.

storage
The cooked dish can be be kept in an airtight container and refrigerated for up to 2 days. Alternatively, it can be frozen for up to 3 months. Defrost overnight in a fridge before reheating until piping hot throughout.

allergens
Wheat (gluten), and celery.

MAKING A BOUQUET GARNI
A delicious flavour enhancer and classic mix is thyme, bayleaf, parsley and celery. Wrap the herbs in the dark green part of a leek and tie tightly with string.

Moroccan lamb tagine

Apricots and lamb make excellent bedfellows in this spicy iron-rich casserole. The long cooking time makes the lamb really tender and, as this recipe will serve 4–6, depending on your appetite, leftovers can be frozen and eaten later if you're not serving all of it at once.

serves 4-6
preparation time 15 minutes
cooking time 2½ hours

1 tbsp olive oil
2 red onions, cut into lengthwise slices
2 cloves of garlic, crushed
700 g lamb, such as neck fillet, cubed
2 level tbsp ground cumin
1 cinnamon stick
2 bay leaves
2 small red chillies
500 ml water
2 heaped tbsp tomato puree
200 g ready to eat apricots

to serve
2 tbsp chopped fresh coriander
150 g low-fat Greek yogurt (optional)

1 Preheat the oven to 160°C, 140°C for fan oven or gas mark 3.
2 Heat the olive oil in a large, preferably non-stick, lidded, heavy-bottomed pan or casserole and add the onions and garlic and fry until the onion is softened.
3 Add the cubed lamb and fry, stirring, for 5 minutes or until the lamb is lightly browned, adding a little more oil to prevent sticking, if necessary.
4 Add the spices and stir around, adding a little water, if needed, to prevent burning.
5 Pour in the rest of the water, the tomato puree and apricots and stir well. Bring the ingredients slowly to the simmering point then cover and transfer the pan or casserole to the oven to cook slowly about 2½ hours, or until the lamb is really tender.
6 Remove the cinnamon stick, bay leaves and chilli and sprinkle over the chopped coriander before serving.

serving suggestions
Eat with low-fat Greek yogurt accompanied by a simple green salad and cous cous.

storage
The cooked dish can be refrigerated for 48 hours and will freeze well for up to 3 months. Thaw in the fridge overnight and reheat in a microwave until piping hot.

allergens
Milk (if served with yogurt).

lamb and pepper koftas with tzatziki

This classic combination is full of pregnancy essentials, from immune boosting vitamin C and zinc for you to essential vitamin B$_{12}$ for your baby. Lamb mince is commonly found in packs of 400 or more grams, so you may only want to make half the recipe and freeze half of the mince, or make up the mixture below and freeze in airtight bags for use another day.

serves 4
preparation time 10 minutes
cooking time 15–20 minutes

for the koftas
1 large slice wholemeal bread (around 50 g)
1 small onion, peeled and quartered
400 g lean lamb mince
2 cloves garlic, peeled
juice of ½ lime
1 tbsp chopped coriander
1 red chilli, (optional), seeds removed and halved
black pepper
1 medium red onion, peeled and quartered
*2 green peppers, seeds removed and cut into
   8 pieces each*

to serve
Tzatziki, page 63

1 Place the bread in a food processor and process until fine.
2 Add the onion, mince, garlic, lime juice, coriander, chilli (if using) and pepper and process until combined.
3 Turn the mixture onto a clean chopping board and divide into 12.
4 Form each into an oval shape.
5 Preheat a grill and lightly oil 4 skewers.
6 Thread the onion and pepper piecess and lamb koftas alternately on each kebab stick.
7 Line a baking sheet or the grill tray with some foil and place the kebabs on it.
8 Grill for 10-15 minutes, turning the kebabs often until the juices of the koftas run clear.
9 Meanwhile prepare the tzatziki.

serving suggestions
Eat with warmed wholemeal pitta bread and the Tzatziki.

storage
The cooked dish is not suitable for storage, but the minced mixture, prepared up through step 2, can be frozen in an airtight container for 1 month. Defrost in the fridge overnight and continue from step 3 of the recipe.

allergens
Milk (yogurt), gluten (bread).

crab linguine

When time is short, we often reach for pasta, but rather than a creamy or tomato sauce, why not try this light sauce combining crab and asparagus with a little lemon boost. Asparagus is a great source of folic acid, but this is easily destroyed so don't overcook it! If you prefer a different vegetable, slice a small trimmed leek, and of course you can always swap crab for a can of tuna, although the latter contains very little omega 3.

serves 1
preparation time 5 minutes
cooking time 15 minutes

75 g linguine or other long pasta
1 tbsp olive oil
1 clove garlic
80 g (approx 4 spears) asparagus, trimmed into
   1-cm slices
50 ml dry white wine
75 g mixed brown and white crab, canned or fresh
1 tsp lemon juice
1 tbsp chopped parsley

1 Cook the pasta according to the packet instructions.
2 Meanwhile, in a small saucepan, heat the oil and add the garlic and asparagus, cooking gently for 2–3 minutes without browning.
3 Add the wine and allow to simmer very gently for around 5 minutes until the asparagus is just tender. (The wine will be dealcoholised.)
4 Then add the crab, lemon juice and parsley.
5 Drain the pasta and place in a serving bowl. Toss with the crab mixture and serve at once.

serving suggestions
Accompany with a mixed salad.

allergens
Wheat (gluten), shellfish.

crab cakes with watercress and orange salad

Crab is a good source of omega 3 fatty acids and iodine, with the brown meat containing much more than the white. The watercress and orange salad are served with a piquant dressing — all of which boosts the vitamin C and A content too.

serves 2
preparation time 15 minutes
cooking time 15 minutes

150 g mashed potatoes
100 g crab, either canned or in a pot, brown, white or mixed
2 spring onions, finely chopped
1 tbsp parsley, finely chopped
black pepper
1 tbsp sesame seeds
1 large slice wholemeal bread or 25–30g wholemeal breadcrumbs
1 egg, beaten
vegetable oil for frying

for the salad
1 large orange, peeled and cut into segments
60 g watercress, washed and trimmed into small sprigs

for the dressing
2 tbsp freshly squeezed orange juice
1 tbsp olive oil
1 tbsp wine or sherry vinegar
pinch of sugar

1 Place the mashed potatoes and crab in a bowl and add the onions and parsley. Stir to combine and divide into four equal portions. Shape each portion into a large patty, using flour, if necessary, to prevent your hands sticking.
2 Process the bread to make crumbs and stir in the sesame seeds. Pour into a shallow bowl.
3 Beat the egg and pour into a shallow bowl.
4 Carefully dip each patty into the beaten egg, ensuring it is covered, then lift into the breadcrumbs. Pat these on so the patty's entire surface is covered before transferring it to a clean chopping board.
5 Heat 2 tbsp oil in a non stick frying pan and cook the crab cakes, in batches if necessary, until the crumbs are golden on one side, then turn over and continue cooking until the cakes are piping hot through and golden brown on the outside.
6 Meanwhile make the salad by combining the orange segments with the watercress and prepare the dressing.
7 Pouring over the dressing and serve the dressed salad with the hot crab cakes.

storage
The crab cakes are best served at once, but could be refrigerated before frying for up to 24 hours in a airtight container. Once dressed, the salad must be eaten at once.

allergens
Wheat (gluten), eggs, shellfish.

VARIATION
You may like to swap the orange for pink grapefruit, and watercress for rocket. If you don't like crab, used flaked smoked mackerel.

Greek style tomato and haddock

An extremely simple and nutritious supper dish, all this needs is a few new potatoes, or some crusty bread as accompaniments. You can use any type of white fish. If you don't like the skin, ask the fishmonger to remove it for you, or use the technique described below.

serves 2
preparation time 5 minutes
cooking time 20 minutes

250 g sustainably sourced white fish fillet, such as
   haddock, plaice or pollack, washed
400 g large ripe tomatoes
handful of basil leaves, torn
2 tbsp Greek olive oil
black pepper, to taste

FOOD SAFETY
Use a separate board to prepare the raw fish. If you are using frozen fish, thaw it in the fridge and ensure it does not drip on other foods.

1 Preheat the oven to 200°C, 180°C for fan oven or gas mark 6
2 Slice the tomatoes and lay in the base of an ovenproof container; sprinkle with half of the basil leaves.
3 Skin the fish if you like or leave with the skin on. Dry with kitchen paper and fold in half. Place on top of the tomatoes and add the remaining basil.
4 Drizzle the oil on top, and grind over some black pepper.
5 Bake for 20 minutes or until the fish just flakes when prodded with a fork. Serve at once making sure to add all the cooking juices.

serving suggestions
Eat with new potatoes or crusty bread, and a side salad.

allergens
Fish.

HOW TO SKIN A FLAT FISH
You will need a sharp cook's knife and a clean chopping board. Lay the fish, skin side down on the board, and press the tail end firmly with your fingers. Place the knife just beyond your fingers at a slight angle away from you and press rather than cut — you should go through the flesh but not the skin. Once you have made this cut, you should be able to push

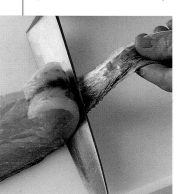

the knife away from you, using a sawing motion if needed as you hang onto the tail. The skin will 'peel' away. If you accidentally cut through the flesh, just begin again from the other end.

potato-topped creamy fish pie

A traditional nursery staple, fish pie is mild in flavour, high on nutrients and slips down easily, making it a meal for days when you are a bit off colour. Later on in pregnancy, make a few to freeze when you are in the mood, so you have some available for when you are breastfeeding, as it provides plenty of calcium too.

serves 4
preparation time 20 minutes
cooking time 20–25 minutes

450 ml semi-skimmed milk
2 bay leaves
400g skinned white fish fillets, e.g. sustainably
  sourced cod, haddock, pollack or hake
150 g cooked shelled prawns
20 g olive spread
30 g plain flour
50 ml single cream
100 g petit pois, thawed
1 tbsp chopped parsley

for the mashed potato topping
700 g potatoes, peeled and quartered
1–2 tbsp milk
pinch of salt (optional)

1 Preheat the oven to 180°C, 160°C for fan oven or gas mark 5.
2 Pour the milk into a shallow saucepan or frying pan and add the bay leaves and fish.
3 Heat very gently to poach the fish, not allowing the milk to get too hot.
4 Meanwhile, prepare the mashed potatoes, by steaming or boiling the potatoes until tender then mashing with the milk and salt, if used.
5 When the fish flakes easily when tested with a fork, carefully lift it out and spread out in a 20 x 20 cm lightly oiled ovenproof dish. Add the cooked prawns.
6 Remove the bay leaves and drain the milk into a jug for use in the sauce.
7 Heat the spread in a saucepan and stir in the flour, cooking for 30 seconds or so before gradually adding the poaching milk, stirring constantly until the sauce has thickened.
8 Add the cream, peas and parsley and pour the mixture over the fish then spoon the potatoes over.
9 Bake for 25-30 minutes until golden brown.

serving suggestions
Accompany with additional peas or a few carrots.

storage
The cooked dish can be kept in an airtight container and refrigerated for 24 hours. Alternatively, it may be frozen for up to 3 months at the end of step 9. Keep it in its dish and wrap with cling film or foil. Defrost in the fridge overnight and cook as in stage 10, allowing a little longer. It must be piping hot when served.

allergens
Fish, shellfish.

main dishes seafood

sea bass with pomegranate salsa

Cooking fish 'en papillote' is a fantastic way of preserving moisture and minimising fishy cooking odours. Sea bass is a white fish rich in B vitamins especially B_3 and B_{12}, and also contains bone building calcium. Here it is served with a salsa containing pomegranate seeds, which are rich in protective polyphenols.

serves 2
preparation time 10 minutes
cooking time 20 minutes

2 x 140 g fillets sea bass
1 garlic clove, crushed
1 tsp grated ginger root
1 tsp grated lime zest

for the pomegranate salsa
½ tsp grated ginger root
½ tsp grated lime zest
1 tsp fresh coriander (optional)
1 tsp runny honey
1 dessertspoon olive oil
1 tsp lemon juice
100 g pomegranate seeds

1 Preheat the oven to 190°C, 170°C for fan oven or gas mark 6
2 Cut two pieces of baking parchment or foil, each approximately 30 cm square. Lightly oil the foil, if used.
3 Lay each fish fillet on a piece of parchment or foil and sprinkle over the garlic, ginger and lime zest.
4 Fold over the top and sides of the parchment or foil loosely to make a parcel and place on a baking sheet.
5 Cook for 15–20 minutes, or until the fish flakes easily when tested with a fork.
6 Meanwhile, mix together all the ingredients for the salsa in a small bowl.
7 Carefully transfer the fish to a warmed plate and serve at once with the salsa.

serving suggestions
Accompany with Gratin of Potato, *page 139 or new potatoes, and a seasonal green vegetable.*

storage
The cooked dish is not suitable for storage, but the salsa may be kept in an airtight container and refrigerated for up to 2 days. Neither is suitable for freezing.

allergens
Contains: fish.

salmon and asparagus en croûte

Salmon (or trout) is full of pregnancy essentials, especially omega 3's and vitamin D. This very easy recipe uses filo pasty to wrap the fillet, and if you pop in a few asparagus tips, you'll be getting a little folic acid too!

serves 1
preparation time 5 minutes
cooking time 20 minutes

2 sheets of filo pastry
a little vegetable oil or an oil mister
2–3 spears of asparagus,
100 g skinless fillet of salmon or trout
few drops lemon or lime juice (optional)

1 Preheat the oven to 190°C, 170°C for fan oven or gas mark 5
2 Place one sheet of pastry on a clean surface and either brush or spray with oil.
3 Pop the fish in the centre and place the asparagus on top, trimmed to the same size as the fillet.
4 Sprinkle over the lemon juice, if used, and wrap up the parcel, tucking the ends under.
5 Lightly brush or spray the other sheet of filo with oil and place the parcel in the middle; roll up the pastry. Transfer the parcel to a baking sheet and spray or brush again with oil.
6 Bake for 20 minutes or until the parcel is golden brown. Serve at once.

serving suggestions
Accompany with some boiled new potatoes and seasonal vegetables. Add a few more steamed asparagus stems for more folic acid. You may also like to accompany with Piquant Avocado Dip, *page 66,* Lime Dressing, *page 119 or* Tzatziki, *page 63.*

allergens
Wheat (gluten), fish.

> ### COOK'S TIP
> *When wrapping a filo pastry parcel using two sheets of pastry, place the filling on the first sheet and wrap, tucking the ends under. Then place the parcel on the second sheet and wrap so the tucked-under ends of the second sheet are opposite those of the first.*

<salmon and asparagus en croûte with piquant avocado dip

smoked salmon flakes with herbed lentils

This simple warm dish uses ready cooked lentils for speed, and makes a delicious lunch or supper dish. It provides one third of your day's needs for iron and zinc as well as giving you a great boost of omega 3 and vitamin D.

serves 2
preparation time 10 minutes
cooking time 5 minutes

1 large stick celery, finely chopped
250 g sachet of ready cooked puy lentils (or 400 g can of whole lentils, drained)
20 g rocket leaves
30 g watercress
160 g pack hot smoked salmon, skinned and flaked

for the dressing
100 ml reduced fat crème fraiche
1 tbsp horseradish sauce
juice of ½ lemon
grated zest of ½ lemon

1 Place the celery in a small pan of boiling water and cook for 3–4 minutes to just soften. Drain.
2 Warm the lentils in a microwave oven or in a pan with 1 tbsp water to prevent sticking. Stir in the celery. Drain if required before mixing in the roughly chopped rocket and watercress.
3 Make the dressing by combining all the ingredients in a small bowl.
4 Stir the dressing into the lentil mixture and lastly add the salmon flakes. Serve at once.

serving suggestions
Eat with a few cherry tomatoes and, if hungry, a slice of wholemeal bread.

storage
The cooked dish is not suitable for storage, but the sauce may be kept in an airtight container and refrigerated for up to 2 days. Alternatively the sauce may be frozen separately but when reheating it must come to the boil before serving.

allergens
Fish, milk (crème fraîche), celery.

sprats with avocado and cherry tomatoes

Sprats are an inexpensive, highly nutritious small fish, smaller than a sardine but larger than a whitebait. As a sustainable, oil-rich fish they are great in pregnancy but any small fresh sardines will do. The bones are small and soft so can be eaten, which provides you with essential calcium, and they are also a very rich source of vitamin D.

serves 2
preparation time 15 minutes
cooking time 10 minutes

for the sprats
400 g fresh sprats or sardines
1 tbsp flour
1 tsp paprika
vegetable oil for frying

for the avocado and cherry tomato salad
1 medium Hass avocado
juice of ½ lemon or lime
150g cherry tomatoes
1 tbsp chopped parsley

1 Firstly, wash the sprats and with a sharp knife remove the head and tail. Slit open from the head end to remove the insides and discard. Wash again and pat dry on kitchen paper. Continue until all the sprats are cleaned and prepared.
2 Make the salad by chopping the peeled avocado into cubes, tossing in the lemon juice and mixing with the cherry tomatoes and parsley.
3 Place the flour on a shallow plate and mix in the paprika. Dip each fish in a little seasoned flour.
4 Heat a couple tablespoons oil in a non-stick frying pan, and when hot, fry the sprats for 4–5 minutes, turning half way through, until they are tender but slightly crispy. Serve at once with the avocado and tomato salad.

serving suggestions
Eat with wholemeal bread as a light supper or lunch.

allergens
Wheat (gluten), fish.

tuna and vegetable pasta bake

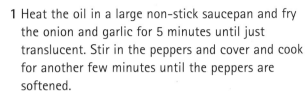

Pasta and cans of tuna and tomatoes are store cupboard staples. Liven then up with some vitamin C-rich peppers and basil to make this nutritious dish that is quick and easy to prepare.

serves 4
preparation time 15 minutes
cooking time 35 minutes

1 tbsp olive oil
1 medium onion, roughly chopped
2 cloves garlic, crushed
2 medium red peppers, quartered, and sliced crosswise
150 g pasta shapes
400 g can chopped tomatoes in juice
handful of basil leaves
2 x 185 g cans tuna in oil, drained
black pepper, optional
100 g Cheddar cheese, grated

1 Heat the oil in a large non-stick saucepan and fry the onion and garlic for 5 minutes until just translucent. Stir in the peppers and cover and cook for another few minutes until the peppers are softened.
2 Meanwhile, boil the pasta according to the packet instructions.
3 Add the canned tomatoes to the vegetable mix and bring to the boil. Turn down the heat, cover and simmer for 5 minutes.
4 Remove from the heat and stir in the basil leaves and drained tuna. Grind over a little pepper.
5 When the pasta has cooked, drain and tip into the base of a large ovenproof dish. Cover with the sauce, mix slightly to combine and sprinkle over the grated cheese.
6 Place in a preheated oven for 20–25 minutes or until the cheese is golden brown and the 'bake' piping hot. Serve at once.

serving suggestions
Eat with steamed broccoli or cauliflower or a large green salad.

storage
The pasta dish can be prepared up to the end of step 5 and chilled for 24 hours or frozen for up to 2 months. Then defrost in the fridge and cook as in step 6. If you prefer to freeze the cooked dish, then defrost it in the fridge and reheat in a microwave until it is piping hot.

allergens
Wheat (gluten), fish, milk (cheese).

main dishes seafood

tuna steaks with sundried tomato crust and lime dressing

Oven cooked with a simple breadcrumb and tomato topping and a lime dressing, this fresh tuna meal is a great source of omega 3 fatty acids and supplies all your vitamin D needs for a day.

serves 2
preparation time 15 minutes
cooking time 20–25 minutes

1 large slice wholemeal bread
50 g sundried tomatoes in oil, drained
1 clove garlic
few basil leaves
2 x 160 g tuna steaks

for the lime dressing
2 rounded tbsp fat-reduced soured cream or crème fraîche,
2 rounded tbsp low-fat Greek yogurt
1 tsp grated lime zest
2 tsp lime juice

1 Preheat the oven to 180°C, 160°C for fan oven or gas mark 5
2 Place the bread, tomatoes, basil and oil in a food processor or blender and blend until fine.
3 Wipe the tuna with clean kitchen paper and place on a lightly oiled baking sheet, and carefully press half the breadcrumb mixture onto each steak.
4 Bake for 20 minutes, or until the tuna flakes easily when tested with a fork.
5 Meanwhile, make the lime dressing by combining all the ingredients in a small bowl.
6 Serve the hot tuna with the dressing.

serving suggestions
Accompany with new potatoes and petit pois, mangetout, green beans or a mixed salad.

storage
The cooked dish is not suitable for storage, but the sauce may be kept in an airtight container and refrigerated for up to 2 days.

allergens
Fish, gluten, milk (creams/ yogurt).

stuffed Portobello mushrooms

These flat, dark, open-capped mushrooms are ideal for stuffing and the simple mixture used here is prepared in a jiffy. The resulting dish provides a host of B vitamins and calcium, all of which are essential for your developing baby.

serves 2
preparation time 5 minutes
cooking time 35 minutes

2 large Portobello or field mushrooms
2 large slices wholemeal bread, torn into pieces
2 cloves garlic
100 g sundried tomatoes in oil, drained
60 g reduced fat Cheddar cheese, grated

1 Preheat the oven to 190°C, 170°C for fan oven or gas mark 5
2 Wipe the cap and stalk of each mushroom with damp kitchen paper and remove the stalk.
3 Place the stalks, garlic and bread in a food processor and blend until fine.

4 Add the drained tomatoes and pulse to chop roughly.
5 Press this mixture into the mushrooms and place them on a lightly oiled baking sheet.
6 Sprinkle the cheese on top of the mushrooms and bake for 30–35 minutes until the mushrooms are tender and the cheese is melted and turning golden.

serving suggestions
Eat with a green salad for lunch, or add baked or new potatoes and roasted vegetables for a delicious supper dish.

allergens
Wheat (gluten).

main dishes vegetarian

butternut squash bake with halloumi and pomegranate

This is a great autumn and winter meal when squash are cheap and pomegranates in season. It provides more than three times your vitamin A needs, and is low in salt, so tuck in. Pomegranates contain many protective antioxidants and, from Biblical times, have been regarded as one of nature's most 'powerful' fruits. Recent studies indicate they may help lower blood pressure, thus reducing your risk of pre-eclampsia.

serves 2-3
preparation time 15 minutes
cooking time 30–35 minutes

1 medium onion, roughly chopped
1 tbsp vegetable oil
400 g butternut squash, peeled and cut into 1-cm cubes
1 medium (approx 250 g) sweet potato, peeled and cubed
60 ml water
150 g frozen leaf spinach, thawed
100 g halloumi, coarsely grated or chopped
seeds from one small pomegranate or 100 g ready-to-eat seeds

1 Preheat the oven to 190°C, 170°C for fan oven or gas mark 5.
2 Heat the oil in a large ovenproof pan and gently fry the onion for 5 minutes until just softening.
3 Add the cubes of squash and sweet potato, stir and cover. Reduce the heat to low and allow the vegetables to sweat for 5 minutes, stirring occasionally to prevent sticking.
4 Pour in the water, re-cover and place the pan in the oven for 20–25 minutes, or until the vegetables are just tender, adding a little more water if necessary.
5 Stir in the spinach and sprinkle over the halloumi. Return the pan to the oven for 10 minutes or until the cheese is melted and starting to brown.
6 Sprinkle with the pomegranate seeds.

serving suggestions
This is a meal in itself but if you like, add a rocket-and-watercress salad.

storage
The cooked dish minus the pomegranate can be stored in an airtight container and refrigerated for up to 24 hours. Reheat until piping hot throughout in a microwave oven, then serve sprinkled with the pomegranate.

allergens
Milk (cheese).

COOK'S TIP
Look out for ready prepared squash and sweet potato cubes to save you time in the kitchen.

VARIATION
For a spicier dish, add 2 tsp toasted cumin seeds at the end of step 2, when the onions are soft and/or a little chilli powder to the vegetables in step 3.

main dishes vegetarian

creamy vegetarian mince

Vegetarian mince made from mycoprotein (quorn) makes an easy supper dish which vegetarians and carnivores alike will enjoy, and which can also be frozen. The addition of peanut butter gives it a creamy texture, and adds antioxidant vitamin E and copper, an essential mineral for the functioning of the vascular system.

serves 4
preparation time 10 minutes
cooking time 20 minutes

1 tbsp olive oil
1 medium onion, finely chopped,
1 clove garlic, crushed,
1 small green pepper, diced
1 tsp ground cumin
300 g vegetarian mince e.g. quorn
2 tbsp tomato puree
400 ml water
3 tbsp peanut butter (about 75 g)

1 Heat the oil in a saucepan and gently fry the onion and garlic for 5 minutes, or until just softening.
2 Add the green pepper and cumin and continue to fry for another minute or so.
3 Stir in the quorn and tomato puree.
4 Lastly pour in the water and bring the mixture to the boil.
5 Stir, cover and reduce heat. Simmer mince for 15 minutes, stirring occasionally, and adding more water, if the mixture seems dry.
6 Stir in the peanut butter and serve.

serving suggestions
Eat with rice and a green vegetable or use as a filling for a jacket potato and accompany with a salad.

storage
This may be kept in an airtight container and refrigerated for 2 days or frozen for 2 months. Thaw in the fridge and reheat until piping hot throughout in a microwave oven.

allergens
Peanuts.

> **VARIATION**
> *For a spicier mix, add ½ teaspoon chilli powder and additional cumin in step 2 and 2 tsps garam masala and 1 tbsp chopped coriander before serving.*

pasta primavera

This quick tasty dish provides two portions of vegetables, plenty of fibre and 50 per cent of your pregnancy requirement of vitamin C. By using wholegrain pasta, you will also increase the amount of iron in this meal to a third of your needs. If you are struggling with nausea, the simple fresh tomato sauce made without onion or garlic, can make it easier for you to be in the kitchen.

serves 2
preparation time 5 minutes
cooking time 20 minutes

2 large ripe tomatoes, about 240 g
1 tbsp olive oil
200 g dry wholegrain fusilli or other pasta shape
80 g broccoli, cut into tiny florets
50 g green beans, trimmed and cut into 2-cm pieces
50 g mangetout, finely sliced

to serve
2 tbsp grated Parmesan or pecorino cheese and
   black pepper

1 Skin the tomatoes, cut into quarters and scoop out the seeds. Chop roughly.
2 Heat the olive oil in a saucepan and add the tomato. Cover and cook very gently for around 15–20 minutes, stirring occasionally until the tomato flesh is really soft.
3 Whilst the sauce is cooking, boil a large pan of water and cook the pasta for 5–6 minutes. Add the broccoli and green beans and cook for a further 2–3 minutes. Finally add the mangetout, cooking for a further minute.
4 Drain the pasta and vegetables and divide between 2 serving dishes, and pour over the sauce.
5 Grind over black pepper and sprinkle with the cheese and serve.

storage
The cooked dish is not suitable for storage, but the sauce may be kept in an airtight container and refrigerated for up to 2 days or frozen. When reheating the sauce, make sure it comes to the boil before serving.

allergens
Wheat (gluten), milk (cheese).

HOW TO SKIN TOMATOES
Score a cross in the base of the tomato and place in a heatproof bowl. Pour over boiling water and leave for one minute. Then lift out with a slotted spoon and using a sharp knife, peel off the skin.

VARIATION
If you prefer to use fresh pasta, cook for the recommended time on the pack and steam the vegetables separately. You may like to add a few torn fresh basil leaves to the sauce.

main dishes vegetarian

roasted baby vegetables with tofu

Silken or firm tofu is made from soya beans and is a versatile food, low in fat and high in protein. It is also a good source of calcium so if you can't tolerate dairy foods, it makes a good alternative to cheese.

serves 2-3
preparation time 10 minutes
cooking time 45 minutes

300 g pack firm tofu
1 tbsp vegetable oil
1 tsp soya sauce
200 g baby aubergine
1 medium red pepper
1 medium red onionc
1 small courgette or 2 baby courgette
2 tbsp olive oil
a few sprigs of thyme, optional

1 Preheat the oven to 200°C, 180°C for fan oven or gas mark 6.
2 Cut the tofu into large cubes and marinate in the vegetable oil and the soy sauce for 10 minutes.
3 Meanwhile, prepare the vegetables: quarter the aubergine, cut the red pepper into slices, slice the red onion lengthwise and halve or quarter the courgette(s).
4 Pour the olive oil into a roasting pan. Add the vegetables and toss them in the oil making sure they are well coated.
5 Bake 40 minutes or until the vegetables are tender.

serving suggestions
Accompany with Almond Rice (page 136), cous cous or tabbouleh.

allergens
Soya.

vegetable pancakes with red pepper sauce

Although it has a long list of ingredients, this nutritious meal is worth making up as a double or triple batch of the pancakes and/or the red pepper sauce to freeze for later use. You can also use ready made pancakes or a tortilla wrap. The complete recipe provides a fantastic boost of vitamin A, as well as supplying over 50 per cent of your needed calcium and vitamin C.

serves 2 (makes 4-6 pancakes depending on the size of your pan)
preparation time 30 minutes
cooking time 30 minutes

for the pancakes
65 g wholemeal flour
65 g white flour
1 large egg
1 tbsp olive oil
200 ml semi skimmed milk
1 tbsp vegetable oil, for cooking

for the red pepper sauce
1 tbsp vegetable oil
1 medium onion, finely chopped
1 medium red pepper, seeded and roughly chopped
400 g can chopped tomatoes in juice

for the vegetables
1 tbsp vegetable oil
1 medium trimmed leek, sliced in half lengthwise then cut into semi circles
1 medium carrot, finely diced
100 g frozen soya beans
100 g frozen sweetcorn

50 g reduced fat Cheddar cheese, grated

1 Prepare the pancakes: place all the ingredients in a blender and process until smooth. You should have a pouring batter; if it is too thick add a little more milk or water. Allow to stand.
2 Prepare the red pepper sauce: Heat the oil in a non-stick saucepan and, over low heat, gently fry the onion until just softened. Add the red pepper and continue to cook gently for 5 minutes, stirring occasionally. Pour in the canned tomatoes, and simmer, covered for 10–15 minutes. or until the vegetables are softened.
3 Meanwhile, in another non-stick pan, heat the oil for the vegetable filling and gently cook the carrot and leek over low heat for 10–15 minutes, or until they are tender. Use a lid to cover and stir occasionally. Stir in the frozen beans and corn and continue cooking over a low heat until all the vegetables are cooked through.
4 To cook the pancakes, put the 1 tbsp of vegetable oil in small jug or egg cup and preferably use a non-stick pan. For each pancake, heat the pan then pour in a dribble of oil. When the oil is hot, pour in some batter, swirling it round to thinly cover the bottom of the pan. Cook until lightly browned on one side then flip over to cook the reverse. Keep the pancakes warm under foil whilst preparing the other ones.
5 When you are ready to serve, fill 2 pancakes per person with the vegetable mixture, and place on a warmed plate. Spoon over some red pepper sauce and sprinkle over some cheese. Serve at once.

serving suggestions
You may like to place the pancakes in a serving dish, cover with the sauce and cheese, then bake for 10–15 minutes until the cheese browns.

storage
The pancakes can be frozen individually layered between greaseproof paper or cling film. The red pepper sauce can also be frozen in an airtight contain and defrosted in the fridge overnight. Alternatively the whole stuffed pancakes may be frozen in an freezer to oven proof dish so that they can be reheated at a later date.

allergens
Wheat (gluten), eggs, milk and cheese.

black eye bean, currant and fresh mint stew

This has to be one of the easiest and most healthy dishes for early in pregnancy. Black eye beans are peculiarly high in folate, and even allowing for nutrient loss in cooking, one portion of this will provide 45 per cent of your dietary needs. The stew also has great credentials for its iron content, and for bone building phosphorus. An all round winner!

serves 2
preparation time 5 minutes
cooking time 20 minutes

1 tbsp olive oil
1 medium onion, roughly chopped
2 medium sticks of celery, finely sliced
2 cloves garlic
400 g can of black eyed beans in water, rinsed and drained
1 tsp cumin
40 g currants
approx 200 ml water
1 tbsp freshly chopped mint
black pepper

1 Heat the oil in a non-stick saucepan and gently fry the onion, celerly and garlic until softened.
2 Add the beans, cumin and currants and stir in the water.
3 Bring to the boil, stir and cover. Reduce the heat to simmering point and cook for 15 minutes or until the vegetables are just tender, adding more water if required.
4 Remove from the heat and stir in the mint and season to taste.

serving suggestions
Eat with rice, pearl barley or cous cous, and a green vegetable or sliced tomatoes.

storage
The cooked dish will freeze for up to 3 months, or can be kept in the refrigerator for 48 hours.

allergens
Celery.

sweet potato and chestnut jalousie

This wonderful party dish, based on a recipe by the well-known chef, Tony Turnbull, is good for you as well as tasty for any vegetarian guests. It is high in vitamin A, and provides more than 50 per cent of your pregnancy needs for copper.

serves 4-6
preparation time 30 minutes
cooking time 45 minutes plus 30–35 minutes

for the roasted vegetables
400 g butternut squash, cut into cubes
400 g sweet potato, peeled and cut into cubes
2 tbsp olive oil

for the remaining filling
1 tbsp vegetable oil
1 medium onion, finely chopped
250 g button mushrooms, wiped and quartered
200 g unsweetened whole chestnuts — frozen or
  vacuum packed, left whole or if large, halved
2 tsp ground cumin
3 level tbsp flour
400 ml vegetable stock or water
1 tbsp mushroom ketchup
2 tbsp parsley, roughly chopped

for the pastry
500 g packet of puff pastry
beaten egg to glaze

1 Preheat the oven to 200°C, 180°C for fan oven or gas mark 6.
2 Place the sweet potato and butternut squash cubes in a clean plastic bag and pour in the olive oil. Shake to coat with the oil and tip onto a baking sheet. Roast for 35–45 minutes, or until the vegetables are tender. Allow to cool; don't turn off the oven.
3 To prepare the remaining filling: heat the oil in a non-stick pan and gently fry the onion until soft, then add the mushrooms. Cover and allow to sweat for 5 minutes, or until they are softened a little.
4 Stir in the cumin, then the chestnuts.

5 Sprinkle over the flour and stir to coat the vegetables. Pour in a little stock to make a thick sauce, then add the remaining stock and the ketchup. Bring to the boil to thicken the sauce, then remove the vegetable mixture from the heat and allow to cool slightly.
6 To prepare the pastry: sprinkle some flour on a clean work surface and cut the pastry in half. Roll out each pastry half as thinly as you can making two rectangles, one slightly larger than the other but both approximately 20 x 30 cm.
7 Place the smaller rectangle of pastry on a lined baking sheet.
8 Mix together the cooled squash and sweet potato with the mushroom mixture and add the parsley. Spoon onto the pastry rectangle on the baking sheet, leaving a 3-cm border all around. Brush this border with water.
9 Using a sharp knife, cut diagonal slashes in the other pastry rectangle, leaving a 3-cm border round the edge. Carefully pick up the pastry on a rolling pin and place on top of the filling. Press the border edges together, trimming off any extra pastry.
10 Brush lightly with the beaten egg and bake for 30–35 minutes until the pastry is risen and golden.

serving suggestions
Because of the double cooking method there is little vitamin C in this dish so serve with steamed broccoli or mangetout, or a watercress and orange salad.

storage
For best results serve at once, but the cooked dish may be refrigerated for 48 hours in an airtight container, and reheated in a conventional oven until piping hot.

allergens
Wheat (gluten), eggs, nuts.

main dishes vegetarian

tarka dhal

My version of this Indian classic is healthy comfort food. Lentils or dried peas are a good source of iron, as are the curry spices.

serves 4
preparation time 5 minutes
cooking time 30 minutes

300 g red lentils, washed
700 ml cold water
5 cardamon pods
2 bayleaves
2 tbsp vegetable oil
1 medium onion, finely chopped
3 cloves garlic, crushed
1 tsp cumin,
1tsp turmeric
2 tsp coriander
pinch of salt
black pepper

1 Place the lentils in a saucepan and cover with the water. Add the bayleaves and cardamom pods and bring to the boil. Stir, reduce the heat and allow to simmer until the lentils are softened, about 30 mnutes, adding more water if required.
2 Meanwhile, in a separate pan, heat the oil and fry the onion and garlic, until softened.
3 Add the cumin, turmeric and coriander and fry for a minute before removing the pan from the heat.
4 When the lentils are cooked, stir in the fried onions, season to taste, remove the bayleaves and serve.

serving suggestions
For a 'hotter' version add 1 tbsp each garam marsala and chopped coriander before serving. Eat with Almond Rice (page 136), sliced tomatoes and a green vegetable.

storage
The dahl can be refrigerated in an airtight container for 2 days or frozen for 2 months. Thaw well at room temperature and reheat until piping hot.

water chestnut and cashew nut stir fry

Cashew nuts may seem an unlikely source of iron, but even a small portion provides you with a good supply of the mineral. Iron absorption is facilitated by the vitamin C supplied by the peppers, making this very quick dish a pregnancy winner.

serves 2
preparation time 5 minutes
cooking time 10 minutes

60 g plain cashew nuts,
2 plain noodle nests (around 75 g each)
1 tbsp rapeseed oil
1 sachet (70 g) water chestnuts, drained and sliced
300 g bag mixed pepper stir fry
1–2 tbsp water.
1 tbsp dry sherry
2 tsp reduced salt (sodium) soy sauce

1 Toast the cashew nuts in a hot oven (200°C, 180°C fan oven or gas mark 6) for a few minutes until lightly browned, or dry fry in a non-stick pan over a low heat on the hob.
2 Meanwhile, place the dry noodle nests in a bowl and pour over boiling water and leave to stand for 5 minutes.
3 Heat the oil in a wok or large frying pan, preferably non-stick, and stir-fry the water chestnuts and vegetable mix for 4 to 5 minutes, adding a little water if they begin to stick to the pan.
4 Stir in the cooked noodles, sherry and soy sauce and once combined, sprinkle over the cashew nuts.

allergens
Wheat (gluten), nuts (cashews).

Brazil nut burgers

This recipe is very simple and versatile — use different types of nuts or breads
to ring the changes.

serves 4
preparation time 5 minutes
cooking time 30 minutes

100 g Brazil nuts
2 large spring onions, chopped
2 slices white bread
1 egg, separated
1 red pepper, diced
salt and black pepper, to taste
oil, for greasing

1 Preheat the oven to 180°C, 160°C for fan oven or gas mark 4.
2 Place the brazil nuts, spring onions and bread in a food processor and whizz until well chopped.
3 Add the egg yolk and red pepper and mix well.
4 Season to taste. If the mixture needs more liquid to bind it, add the egg white.
5 Form the mixture into 4 even-sized balls and press down to form burgers about 1–2 cm thick.
6 Place the burgers on a greased baking sheet and cook for 25–30 minutes, or until the burgers are slightly browned and crunchy on the outside.

serving suggestions
Serve in a toasted bun with some tomato relish and a side salad or baked new potatoes.

storage
The cooked burgers can be frozen once cold, and reheated until piping hot in the microwave.

allergens
Gluten (wheat), eggs, nuts (Brazils).

VARIATION
Use ciabatta rolls instead of burger buns for a change.
Warm them in the oven first to crisp up the crust

main dishes vegetarian

kachumbari

This vitamin C-rich salad from East Africa is a great accompaniment to grilled meat. The key to making a success of this salad is a very sharp knife or mandolin as everything needs to be sliced very finely.

serves 4
preparation time 10 minutes
cooking time 0 minutes

3–4 large ripe tomatoes
1 small green pepper
1 small red onion,
pinch of salt
juice of 1 small lemon (about 20 ml)
1 tbsp chopped coriander

1 Wash the tomatoes and slice as finely as you can.
2 Remove the stalk and seeds from the pepper, quarter and slice finely.
3 Peel the onion, halve and slice very finely.
4 Mix the 3 vegetables in a bowl with a pinch of salt and pour over the lemon juice.
5 Lastly stir in the coriander, cover and chill for at least 15 minutes to allow the salt to draw some of the juices from the salad vegetables.

serving suggestions
Use to accompany grilled meats or steaks of all kinds.

storage
The salad may be kept in an airtight container and refrigerated for 24 hours.

two pear salad

This cool salad will make a welcome change from cooked vegetables in the winter months, when pear and avocado are widely available. The avocado provides healthy monounsaturated fats as well as vitamin E.

serves 2
preparation time 10 minutes
cooking time 0 minutes

for the dressing
1 tbsp runny honey
2 tbsp olive oil
grated zest of one lime
1 tbsp lime juice

for the salad
1 medium ripe avocado pear
1 large ripe pear, e.g. conference
60 g cos lettuce

1 Firstly make the dressing by whisking together all the ingredients in a large bowl.
2 Peel the avocado, remove the stone and cut into cubes. Stir these into the dressing to prevent browning.
3 Cut the other pear into quarters, and remove the core. Cube and add to the bowl. If the skin is tough, you may like to peel it first.
4 Shred the lettuce and place in a serving dish.
5 Spoon the pears and dressing over the lettuce and serve at once.

serving suggestions
Use to accompany grilled poultry, or add a handful of toasted walnuts and serve with bread as a main course.

ginger and orange slaw

A tangy salad containing ginger to help combat nausea, this slaw utilises winter produce with its high vitamin C content to keep winter bugs at bay. Enjoy it with baked potatoes, cold meat (including left-over turkey), or on its own with a few added nuts.

serves 3
preparation time 10 minutes
cooking time 0 minutes

2-cm piece fresh ginger root, finely grated.
1 tbsp lemon juice
1 tbsp runny honey
¼ small red cabbage (about 150 g)
1 stick of celery, washed and trimmed (about 30 g)
1 medium carrot, peeled, topped and tailed (about 80 g)
1 large orange (about 200 g)

1 Mix the grated ginger, lemon juice and honey together in a large mixing bowl.
2 Using a mandolin, or food processor, finely slice the cabbage and celery and stir into the bowl.
3 Roughly grate the carrot and add to the other ingredients.
4 Lastly, using a small sharp knife, peel the orange. Then hold the orange above the bowl to catch any drips, and cut away the flesh of each segment, halve, and add to the salad.
5 Stir all the ingredients together well and serve, or cover with cling film and chill until required.

serving suggestions
Great with roasted chicken thighs and a baked potato; or add a few dry roast peanuts and have as a snack.

storage
The salad will keep refrigerated for 24 hours in an airtight container.

allergens
Celery.

vegetables and side dishes

131

curly kale with garlic cherry tomatoes

Curly kale is an often overlooked vegetable, rich in vitamins A and C, which will help boost your immune system and keep 'bugs' at bay. If you haven't tried this vegetable before, prepare this simple recipe and you'll be suprised at how delicious it can be.

serves 2
preparation time 5 minutes
cooking time 15 minutes

1 tbsp olive oil
150 g cherry tomatoes, washed and halved
2 cloves garlic, crushed
120 g curly kale, washed and roughly chopped
black pepper

1 Heat the oil in a small saucepan and gently cook the tomatoes and garlic, stirring frequently.
2 Meanwhile wash and drain the curly kale.
3 When the tomatoes are softened, add the kale to the pan, stir well and bring to the boil. Allow to simmer for a few minutes until the kale has wilted and is just tender.
4 Remove from the heat and grind over some black pepper, and serve at once

serving suggestions
Good as an accompaniment to grilled meat or poultry.

broccoli with almonds

When purple sprouting broccoli is in season (late winter to spring in the UK), it is a fantastically good source of folate, which is especially important in early pregnancy. Out of season use tender-stem or regular broccoli, remembering to steam it till just tender to preserve that vital B vitamin. For that reason, you need to serve it right away not store it.

serves 2
preparation time 5 minutes
cooking time 10 minutes

230 g pack purple sprouting broccoli florets or other broccoli, washed
1 tbsp olive oil
2 cloves garlic, crushed
50 g sundried tomatoes in oil, drained
25 g flaked and toasted almonds

1 Steam the broccoli until just tender.
2 Meanwhile heat the oil in a small pan and gently fry the garlic until just soft, without browning.
3 Roughly chop the tomatoes and stir into the garlicky oil.
4 When the broccoli is cooked, lift onto a serving plate and top with the tomato mixture. Sprinkle over the toasted almonds.

serving suggestions
This tastes great with grilled chicken thighs or plain fish.

allergens
Nuts (almonds).

spinach with currants and pine nuts

Spinach is a great source of beta carotene which your body converts to vitamin A which it is particularly useful in the development of your baby's lungs. Here the spinach is cooked Spanish-style with pine nuts and currants, which enhance its nutritional credentials further with vitamin E and healthy monounsaturated fats. It should be served right away (not stored) for the maximum retention of vitamins.

serves 2
preparation time 5 minutes
cooking time 10 minutes

2 tbsp pine nuts (about 30 g)
300 g spinach leaves, well washed and drained
1 tbsp olive oil
2 tbsp currants (50 g)
nutmeg

1 Toast the pine nuts in a dry frying pan until they are lightly browned or in a preheated oven (200°C, 180°C for fan oven or gas mark 6.) Take care that they don't become overdone.
2 Meanwhile, place the drained spinach in a large saucepan and cook until it has all wilted. You won't need additional water for this.
3 When the spinach has all wilted, drain off the excess liquid, and place in a serving dish.
4 Grate over some nutmeg, pour over the olive oil, and stir in the currants and pine nuts. Serve hot at once.

serving suggestions
Delicious with any grilled or roasted meat, fish or poultry, or stews.

COOK'S TIP
Not actually a nut but a seed of the pine tree, pine nuts are high in protein. While they can be eaten raw, toasting them brings out their buttery flavour and adds a little extra crunch.

vegetables and side dishes

134

roast beet and butternut squash

Beetroot is rich in folate and butternut squash in beta-carotene, which your body turns to vitamin A. Both nutrients are pregnancy essentials and you and your baby will have at least one quarter of your day's needs in this easy, nutritious side dish.

serves 2
preparation time 10 minutes
cooking time 45 minutes

2 medium fresh beetroot (approx. 250 g)
250 g butternut squash, cut into large cubes
1 medium red onion, cut into wedges
2 tbsp olive oil
chopped parsley to garnish.

1 Preheat the oven to 200°C, 180°C for fan oven or gas mark 6.
2 Using plastic gloves to prevent your hands from staining, peel the beetroot and cut each into 8 wedges. Place in a medium size roasting tin.
3 Add the squash and onion and drizzle over the olive oil. Give the tin a good shake or stir to coat the vegetables with the oil.
4 Roast until the vegetables are tender — around 40–45 minutes.
5 Serve sprinkled with a little parsley.

serving suggestions
Ideal with roasted or grilled meat, fish or poultry. Try using any left overs in Barley and Roasted Vegetable Salad with Pumpkin Seeds, *page 71.*

storage
The roasted vegetables can be refrigerated for 24 hours and used in salads. They are not suitable for reheating or freezing.

green chilli edamame

Providing vitamin C as well as fibre, soya or edamame beans make a welcome change to frozen peas. Here they are stir-fried with green peppers, chilli and spring onion for an Oriental-style vegetable accompaniment.

serves 2
preparation time 5 minutes
cooking time 5 minutes

2 tsps vegetable oil
½ medium green pepper (80–100 g), sliced
3 spring onions, trimmed and cut into 1-cm slices
1 green chilli, finely chopped
100g soya/ edamame beans, defrosted, if frozen

1 Heat the oil in a non-stick wok or frying pan
2 Lightly fry the pepper and onions for 2–3 minutes before adding the chilli then beans.
3 Stir-fry for 3–4 minutes, or until the vegetables are just tender and piping hot. Serve at once.

serving suggestions
Use to accompany Chinese Pork with Plums (page 97), tuna steaks, or any other hot savoury dish of your choice.

allergens
Soya (edamame).

almond rice

Adding a few flaked almonds to rice adds a nice crunch, but unfortunately won't add significant amounts of nutrients. However, almonds do provide antioxidant vitamin E, and a little calcium and iron, and this dish makes a change from plain boiled rice!

----

serves 2
preparation time 15 minutes
cooking time 15 minutes

----

1 tbsp vegetable oil
½ onion (about 50 g)
100 g basmati rice, rinsed well and drained (see
   page 83)
275 ml boiling water
pinch of salt
1 bayleaf
35 g flaked almonds, toasted

1 Add the oil to a pan and when hot, fry the onion
   until lightly browned.
2 Stir in the rinsed rice and water.
3 Add salt and the bayleaf and bring to the boil.
4 Cover the pan, lower the heat and simmer for 10
   minutes, or until all the water is absorbed.
5 Remove the bayleaf and fluff up the rice with a fork.
6 Sprinkle over the almonds before serving,

serving suggestions
Eat with Tarka Dhal, *page 128, tagines or curried dishes.*

allergens
Nuts (almonds).

orange and mint cous cous

Shop-bought flavoured cous cous is often highly salty, but you can easily make your own salt-free tasty cous cous. and cheaper, too. Choose the wholegrain version, if possible. This version uses a little boiling water to start the grains fluffing up, then unsweetened orange juice to provide vitamin C.

serves 2
preparation time 5 minutes
cooking time 0 minutes

100 g cous cous, preferably wholegrain
50 ml boiling water
150 ml unsweetened orange juice
8 large mint leaves, finely chopped

1 Place the cous cous in a heatproof bowl and pour over the boiling water, and allow to stand for 2–3 minutes.
2 Pour over the orange juice, and allow to stand for a further 5 or so minutes, or until all the juice has been absorbed.
3 Fork in the mint leaves and serve at once.

serving suggestions
Use to accompany goulash, stews or any meal where you may use rice. You may also add a spoonful of chopped seeds or nuts and a handful of dried fruit to make a delicious salad with any left overs.

storage
The cous cous can be refrigerated for 24 hours, but is not suitable for freezing.

allergens
Gluten (wheat).

herbed barley

Pearl barley is a great little grain, low on the glycaemic index, full of fibre and a great base for salads and soups as well as served as an alternative to rice, pasta or potatoes. This recipe serves two, but if you make more, the remainder can be used for the delicious *Barley and Roasted Vegetable Salad with Pumpkin Seeds* on page 71.

serves 2
preparation time 5 minutes
cooking time 40–45 minutes

100 g pearl barley
200 ml low salt vegetable stock
15 g finely chopped parsley

1 Place the barley and stock in a small saucepan and bring to the boil.
2 Stir, cover and reduce the temperature. Simmer gently until all the stock has been absorbed and the grains are just tender, around 45 minutes.
3 Remove from the heat and stir in the chopped parsley and serve at once.

serving suggestions
A great side dish for a casserole or goulash. Try using any left overs in Barley and Roasted Vegetable Salad with Pumpkin Seeds, *page 71.*

storage
The barley is best served soon after making, but can be kept in the fridge for 24 hours and used to make salads.

allergens
Gluten (barley).

vegetables and side dishes

quinoa and sunflower seeds

Quinoa contains lots of iron and zinc, and is gluten free. It cooks fairly quickly and can make a delicious side dish to rival rice. It isn't rich in vitamins B or C, which suffer from reheating, so it is an ideal grain to cook in bulk and freeze in individual portions to heat up later.

serves 2
preparation time 5 minutes
cooking time 15–20 minutes

120 g quinoa
360 ml water
1 tbsp sunflower seeds
2 tsp olive oil
black pepper
pinch of salt

1 Place the quinoa in a saucepan and pour over the water. Bring to the boil, stir and cover. Simmer gently, checking periodically until all the water has been absorbed.
2 Meanwhile, toast the sunflower seeds either in a dry frying pan on the hob or in a preheated oven (200°C, 180°C for fan assisted or gas mark 6) until just lightly browned and crisp.
3 When the quinoa is cooked, stir in the olive oil, and season.
4 Place in a serving bowl and sprinkle over the seeds. Serve hot.

serving suggestions
Good with roasted or grilled meat, fish or poultry or stews.

storage
The quinoa can be refrigerated for up to 48 hours, or frozen in small batches for up to 2 months. Defrost in the fridge and reheat in a microwave oven until piping hot.

hot potato salad

My much healthier version of potato salad, uses herbs and olive oil rather than mayonnaise and is served hot to retain vitamin C. The fresh herbs also add beneficial phytonutrients for you and your baby, as well as being a good replacement for salt.

serves 2
preparation time 5 minutes
cooking time 20 minutes

300 g new or salad potatoes, scrubbed clean and halved if large
2 tbsp olive oil
3 spring onions, cut into 1-cm slices
10 g mixed herbs such as parsley and mint, finely chopped

1 Steam or boil the potatoes until just tender, and drain.
2 Whilst the potatoes are still hot, pour over the olive oil and toss with the herbs and onions. Serve right away

serving suggestions
Use to accompany roasted meat or poultry or grilled fish.

storage
The salad can be cooled and refrigerated overnight but is best and most nutritious served hot.

gratin of potato

This is a good accompaniment to an oven cooked casserole, as it can bake alongside and be ready at the same time. Instead of the usual double cream, this is made with skimmed milk, keeping the fat content down and increasing the amount of calcium, so one portion provides over a quarter of your daily calcium requirement.

serves 2
preparation time 10 minutes
cooking time 1–1½ hours

300 g 'old' potatoes such as Desiree or Maris Piper
150 ml skimmed milk
pinch of salt
pinch grated nutmeg
25 g Cheddar cheese, grated
few fresh rosemary sprigs, optional

1 Preheat the oven to 160°C, 140°C for fan oven or gas mark 3. Oil a small ovenproof gratin dish.
2 Peel the potatoes, and slice as thinly as you can, using a mandolin if you have one.
3 Rinse the potatoes well and pat dry on a clean kitchen towel.
4 Arrange the potato slices in layers in the dish.
5 Season the milk with salt, if used, pepper and nutmeg and pour over the potato.
6 Cover loosely with foil, place on a baking sheet in case of spillage and place in the oven for around 1 hour.
7 Remove from the oven and pierce with a sharp knife to test if the potatoes are tender. Return for longer if not soft or if now tender, sprinkle over the cheese and return to the oven, with rosemary sprigs, if using, but without the foil to crisp.

COOK'S TIP
You can use new potatoes to make this gratin, which will increase the vitamin C content. Or if you like add crushed garlic when layering the potatoes.

serving suggestions
Use to accompany casseroles or tagines, or grilled meat or poultry with sauce.

storage
The gratin can be reheated although the vitamin content will be reduced. Refrigerate for up to 48 hours and reheat in a microwave oven until piping hot.

allergens
Milk.

vegetables and side dishes

orange and pomegranate salad

Very rich in vitamin C, this refreshing dessert works well in the winter months when both fruits are abundant. Oranges are also a great source of folate, which is needed early on.

serves 2
preparation time 10 minutes
cooking time 0 minutes

2 medium-large oranges
100 g pomegranate seeds
2 tbsp unsweetened orange juice, optional
1 tbsp runny honey
2-3 mint leaves, finely chopped
Seeds from 3 cardamon pods, ground, or pinch of
  ground cardamon
Greek-style yogurt (fat-free), to serve

1 Using a amall sharp knife, slice off the top and bottom of the orange. Set it on its base and cut off a strip of peel from top to bottom, removing the white pith. Continue all around the orange until it is completely pith free. Then lay on its side and cut into thin slices saving the juice.
2 Place the orange slices and pomegranate seeds in a serving dish.
3 Mix the honey with the saved juice, or use ready-made juice if your oranges were not juicy.
4 Stir in the mint leaves and cardamom, and pour over the fruit.
5 Serve at once, adding a dollop of yogurt, or cover with cling film and chill until required.

storage
Best served at once, but will keep in the fridge for 24 hours, with some vitamin C and folic acid loss.

raspberry and pomegranate jelly

Raspberries are a wonderful source of vitamin C as well as flavones and phenols, which boost your immune system. Mums-to-be who have pregnancy diabetes can use the natural sweetener, xylitol.

serves 4
preparation time 15 minutes
cooking time 0 minutes

1 x 11 g sachet gelatine
30 g caster sugar or xylitol
50 ml red fruit cordial, e.g grenadine or cassis or
  sugar-free cordial
150 g fresh raspberries
150 g pomegranate seeds

1 Make the jelly by pouring 50 ml of hot, but not boiling water into a measuring jug, and sprinkle over the gelatine. Allow to stand for a couple of minutes then stir to dissolve the gelatine.
2 Dissolve the sugar or xylitol in 100 ml cold water and add to the measuring jug of dissolved gelatine.
3 Add the cordial and enough water to make up 400 ml of jelly.
4 Place the raspberries and pomegranate seeds in a serving dish. Pour over the jelly mixture and place in the fridge to set for at least a couple of hours

serving suggestions
Accompany with vanilla ice cream, or a spoonful of low-fat Greek yogurt.

storage
The jelly can be refrigerated for 2-3 days. It is not suitable for freezing.

strawberry mousse

Home-made mousses and soufflés are usually off limits in pregnancy because they use raw egg white. However, if you use dried egg white, which is pasteurised, you can enjoy light desserts without worry. Here, dried egg white is used to make a meringue into which you simply fold strawberry puree and fromage frais. When strawberries are at their peak, this low-fat, vitamin C-rich dish will slip down easily.

serves 4
preparation time 10 minutes
cooking time 0 minutes

1 x 8 g sachet dried egg white
60 ml warm water
50 g caster sugar
400 g strawberries, wiped, hulled and halved;
   reserve a few for decoration
300 g low-fat fromage frais

FOOD SAFETY
Do not use raw egg white for this recipe.

MAKING MERINGUE
To check that your egg whites are the right consistency, lift your whisk. The mixture below should stand up without curling over.

1 Place the egg white in a large mixing bowl and stir in 2 tbsp of the warm water. Mix well to dissolve then pour in the remaining water and whisk until the egg white is light and forms peaks.
2 Add the sugar and continue whisking until you have a thick glossy meringue.
3 Puree the strawberries in a blender, and carefully fold into the meringue.
4 Fold in the fromage frais and then pour the mousse into 4 individual serving dishes.
5 Chill until required, then serve topped with the reserved strawberries.

serving suggestions
You can eat it with a plain sweet biscuit.

storage
The mousse can be kept covered in cling film in the fridge for 2 days. It is not suitable for freezing.

allergens
Eggs.

desserts and baking

dried fruit salad

Great for a simple dessert, this dish is rich in fibre and one portion provides around 20 per cent of your day's need for iron. Choose different dried fruit but bear in mind that figs, apricots and raisins are higher in iron than prunes, pears or apples, and figs are best for calcium. It also makes a terrific breakfast.

serves 3
preparation time 5 minutes
chilling time overnight

75 g dried figs, halved if large, and stalk removed
75 g dried prunes
30 g raisins
60 g dried apricots
10 g dried apple pieces
250 ml unsweetened orange juice
1 cinnamon stick or vanilla pod, or both (optional)
plain yogurt, to serve

1 Place all the fruit in a bowl and pour over the juice.
2 Add the cinnamon or vanilla, if used.
3 Cover with cling film and refrigerate overnight.
4 Remove the cinnamon stick and/or vanilla pod before serving and top with a dollop of yogurt.

storage
This salad will keep in the fridge for 2-3 days.

summer fruit compote

Rich in vitamin C and protective polyphenols, this compote is an easy way to have two of your five a day in one easy dish.

serves 2
preparation time 5 minutes
cooking time 5 minutes

380 g pack frozen mixed summer fruit, thawed or
150 g blackberries
90 g blackcurrants
20 g redcurrants
120 g raspberries
50 g caster sugar or xylitol

1 If using frozen fruit, place the defrosted fruit in a small saucepan and add the sugar or xylitol.
2 Bring very gradually to simmering point, stir to dissolve the sugar and then remove from the heat.
3 If using fresh fruit, place all the fruit except the raspberries in a saucepan with the sugar or xylitol. Bring to simmering point, then stir in the raspberries. Remove from the heat.
4 Allow to cool and serve at room temperature, or if you prefer, chill.

serving suggestions
Eat with a spoonful of Greek yogurt.

storage
The compote can be refrigerated in an airtight container for 2-3 days. It can also be frozen for up to 3 months.

> **COOK'S TIP**
> Make a simple fruit coulis by blending the fruit compote and storing it in several freezer bags in the freezer for up to 3 months.

mango and lime dessert

Mangoes are an amazing source of vitamins A and C, which are essential for your baby's eye development, as well as keeping you healthy during pregnancy. This dessert uses calcium-rich tofu which makes this dessert ideal if you can't tolerate dairy foods..

serves 2
preparation time 10 minutes
cooking time 0 minutes

1 ripe, medium-sized mango or 300 g ready
   prepared mango cubes
175 g silken tofu
grated zest of 1 lime
1 tbsp lime juice
½ tsp vanilla essence

1 If using whole mango, peel and cut into cubes.
2 Place all the ingredients in a food processor or
   blender and process until smooth.
3 Spoon into 2 serving dishes, and chill until required.

serving suggestions
Accompany with a 'cigarette russe' biscuit.

storage
This dessert can be refrigerated, covered with cling film for a day or two. It is not suitable for freezing.

allergens
Soya.

DICING A MANGO
Slice the flesh of the two stoneless sections in a lattice pattern, cutting down to the peel but not piercing it. Push the peel inside out with your thumbs. Cut away cubes with a knife.

pears in chocolate sauce

Pears are easily digested and a good source of fibre. They are served here with a chocolate sauce, but if you want a lower fat option, choose a ready-made fruity coulis, or make your own by blending a little of the Summer Fruit Compote (page 142).

serves 2
preparation time 15 minutes
cooking time 45 minutes

2 large ripe pears, which will stand upright in a pan
(e.g. comice)
300 ml grape juice
1 vanilla pod

for the chocolate sauce
(makes sufficient for 3 servings)
50 g plain chocolate with at least 70% cocoa solids
15 g butter
15 g soft brown sugar
50 ml reduced fat single pouring cream

1 Peel the pears carefully leaving the stalk, if present. This can be useful for manoeuvring the pear later.
2 Stand the pears upright in a small saucepan and add the grape juice and vanilla pod. Cover and cook over a very gentle heat for 40–45 minutes, occasionally spooning some of the cooking liquor over the pears.
3 When the pears are tender, remove from the heat and carefully lift into a serving bowl. Discard or reuse the vanilla pod and let the cooking liquor cool to serve with the pears.
4 Meanwhile, whilst the pears are poaching, melt the chocolate and butter in a small bowl over a pan of just simmering water.
6 When they are melted, stir in the sugar until it dissolves, then add the cream.
7 Stir and pour into a small jug.
8 Serve the poached pears with their juice and some chocolate sauce poured over.

storage
The pears, once cooked, can be stored in an airtight container and refrigerated for up to 2 days. The sauce may also be refrigerated. Neither are suitable for freezing.

allergens
Milk (butter and cream).

traditional rice pudding

This minimum-preparation pudding is ideal for days when you may feel a little nauseous and a single portion contains nearly half of your day's needs for calcium.

---

serves 4
preparation time 5 minutes
cooking time 1½–2 hours

---

750 ml semi-skimmed milk
60 g pudding or short grain rice.
50 g caster sugar or xylitol
2–3 strips of lemon zest
whole nutmeg for grating

1 Preheat the oven to 150°C, 130°C for fan oven or gas mark 2
2 Oil an 850-ml ovenproof dish.
3 Mix the rice, milk and sugar or xylitol in the dish, and add the strips of lemon zest.
4 Cover the surface with finely grated nutmeg and bake for 1½–2 hours, or until the pudding has a caramel coloured brown crust and the rice is tender and soft.
5 Serve at once, removing the lemon strips when you find them.

serving suggestions
Accompany with Summer Fruit Compote or Dried Fruit Salad (both on page 142).

storage
The pudding can be covered with cling film and refrigerated for up to 2 days. Reheat in a microwave oven to prevent it drying out. It is not suitable for freezing.

allergens
Milk.

honey-roasted stone fruit

British summer time brings a host of succulent stone fruit. Enjoy a selection roasted with a little runny honey for a boost of vitamin C and an easily digested dessert.

---

serves 2
preparation time 5 minutes
cooking time 15–20 minutes

---

1 medium ripe peach or nectarine
2 medium ripe apricots
2 medium ripe plums
8 cherries, stoned
2 level tbsp runny honey

1 Preheat the oven to 180°C, 160°C for fan oven or gas mark 5
2 Wash the fruit and cut the larger fruits in half. Remove the stones, and cut in half again.
3 Place all the fruit in a small ovenproof dish and drizzle with the honey
4 Bake for 15–20 minutes, or until the fruit is just tender.
5 Serve at once with any cooking juices.

serving suggestions
Top with a dollop of low-fat Greek yogurt.

storage
The fruit can be stored in an airtight container and refrigerated for up to 2 days. It is not suitable for freezing.

baked figs with pistachios and honey yogurt

Fresh figs are a wonderful source of fibre, and make a delicious, inexpensive hot dessert when they are in season. There are several varieties of figs available in the UK — look out for the smaller Brown Turkey or larger Bursa figs from late summer into autumn. Choose fruit which is plump and tender but not soft. Fruit which is not ripe can be ripened on a windowsill for a day or two.

serves 2
preparation time 10 minutes
cooking time 15–20 minutes

1-2 figs per person, (aiming for 80-90 g portion)
2 level tbsp honey
150 g pot thick plain yogurt, e.g. Greek style
20 g unsalted pistachio nuts, roughly chopped.

1 Preheat the oven to 190°C, 170°C for fan oven or gas mark 5.
2 Wash the figs and cut in half from stem to base.
3 Lay the figs in a small ovenproof dish and spoon over the honey. Bake, uncovered for 15–20 minutes so the figs are soft and hot through
4 Remove from the oven and place the figs in 2 serving dishes, saving the honeyed cooking juices.
5 Place the yogurt in a small mixing bowl and stir in the cooking juices. Spoon half next to the figs and sprinkle over the pistachios. Serve at once.

storage
The cooked figs can be stored in the fridge. Make the honeyed yogurt and store separately, but don't add the nuts until serving. Not suitable for freezing.

allergens
Milk (yogurt), nuts (pistachio).

COOK'S TIP
To measure out runny honey accurately, dip the spoon in a cup of very hot water before measuring.

chocolate brioche pudding

A comforting and fluffy bread and butter pudding made with sweet brioche bread and a sweet chocolate egg custard. Adding a few prunes increases sweetness (and fibre content) without the need for much additional sugar.

serves 3
preparation time 10 minutes
cooking time 30–35 minutes

25 g cocoa powder
15 g sugar
250 ml semi skimmed milk
2 medium eggs, beaten
1 tsp vanilla esssence
100 g sliced brioche loaf
50 g ready to eat prunes, roughly chopped

1 Preheat the oven to 180°C, 160°C for fan oven or gas mark 4.
2 Grease a 1-litre capacity oven proof dish
3 Mix the cocoa powder and sugar with a little of the milk until smooth. Add the remaining milk, eggs and vanilla to make a custard mixture.
4 Cut the slices of bread diagonally in half or quarters, depending on the size of your dish. Place a layer in the bottom of the dish, add half the prunes and pour over half of the chocolate mixture. Repeat.
5 Bake until the pudding is light and fluffy and when you insert a knife, the egg custard is no longer runny.

serving suggestions
Top with a spoonful of reduced fat single cream.

storage
The pudding can be kept covered in the fridge for 2-3 days, and if reheated must be piping hot.

allergens
Gluten (wheat), eggs, milk.

COOK'S TIP
A good quality bread, such as brioche (which is egg-rich), gives the best results.

desserts and baking

apple and blackcurrant oat crumble

This simple dessert uses fresh apples and a can of blackcurrants in juice. Canned blackcurrants contain more iron than fresh, and as they are in juice, you don't need to sweeten the apples with sugar.

serves 4
preparation time 10 minutes
cooking time 25–30 minutes

350 g cooking apples (2 medium), peeled
290 g can blackcurrants in juice
1 tsp cornflour
75 g plain white flour
50 g brown sugar
75 g rolled oats
pinch of cinnamon
50 g polyunsaturated spread (not fat reduced)

1 Preheat the oven to 190°C, 170°C for fan oven or gas mark 5. Grease an 1½ litre capacity ovenproof dish
2 Slice the apples into thin slices. Drain the blackcurrants, reserving the juice and place in the dish. Stir the cornflour into the blackcurrant juice then pour over the fruit.
3 Sieve the flour into a mixing bowl, and add the sugar, oats and cinnamon. Rub in the spread until the mixture is all combined.
4 Spoon the crumble topping over the fruit and bake for 25–30 minutes, or until the crumble is golden brown and the apples are tender when you insert a knife. Serve immediately.

serving suggestions
Accompany with custard, some low-fat fromage frais or yogurt, or vanilla ice cream.

storage
The crumble is best served on the day it is made but can be kept in the fridge for 2 days. It can also be frozen for up to 2 months.

allergens
Gluten (oats, wheat).

fruity flapjack

Add zinc to your pregnancy diet in a very palatable way with this flapjack made with pumpkin seeds and figs, both of which are a great source of this essential mineral. One slice will provide you with 15 per cent of your day's need for zinc and 10 per cent of iron.

serves 16
preparation time 15 minutes
cooking time 30-35 minutes

150 g sunflower spread (not reduced fat)
100 g maple syrup
50 g soft brown sugar
100 g dried dates, chopped
100 g figs, chopped
100 g dried apricots, chopped
75 g pumpkin seeds
250 g rolled oats (see tip)

1 Preheat the oven to 190°C, 170°C for fan oven or gas mark 6.
2 Grease a traybake tin, around 24-cm square.
3 Heat the sunflower spread, syrup and sugar in a saucepan over low heat until they are melted, stirring occasionally. Take care not to boil the mixture.
4 Stir in the chopped dates and continue to heat gently for a minute or two to soften the dates.
5 Meanwhile, combine all the remaining dry ingredients in a large mixing bowl.
6 Pour the date syrup mixture into the bowl and stir until all the dry ingredients are coated with the syrup.

7 Spoon into the prepared tin and level the mixture by pressing down with the back of a clean spoon.
8 Bake until the mixture just turns golden, then remove from the oven and allow to cool for a few minutes.
9 Before the mixture sets completely, cut into 16 pieces with a sharp knife and then allow to cool in the tin.
10 When cold, carefully remove the flapjacks and store in an airtight tin until required.

serving suggestions
Eat with a glass of milk or juice.

storage
The flapjacks keep well for up to a week in an airtight container in a cool dry place. They may be frozen for up to 3 months.

allergens
Gluten (oats).

COOK'S TIP
When making flapjacks with lots of extra ingredients you may find the mixture holds together better if you use the less expensive rolled oats as well as or instead of jumbo oats.

desserts and baking

carrot tray bake

- - - - - - - - - - - - - - - - - - -

Whilst one could not claim that eating cake is a pregnancy essential, this cake does at least provide one third of your day's needs of vitamin A, thanks to the carrots it contains. Make one to freeze for when your baby is born and you have lots of admiring visitors — it won't just be the baby they'll be admiring!

serves 16
preparation time 15 minutes
cooking time 35–40 minutes

200 ml vegetable (rapeseed) oil
150 g light muscovado sugar
3 medium eggs
175 g finely grated carrot
100 g wholemeal flour
100 g plain white flour
3 level tsp baking powder
1 level tsp ground cinnamon
50 g walnuts, roughly chopped

for the icing
30 g unsalted butter
40 g full-fat cream cheese or mascarpone
1 tbsp lemon juice
150 g icing sugar, sieved

1 Preheat the oven to 180°C, 160°C for fan oven or gas mark 4
2 Line an 24-cm or 25-cm square baking tin with greaseproof paper and oil lightly
3 Pour the oil into a large bowl, then whisk in the sugar and eggs until the mixture is paler and the volume has increased.
4 Fold in the carrots.
5 Sieve the flours, baking powder and cinnamon together and fold into the mixture, adding any bran which has remained in the sieve.
6 Lastly, fold in the walnuts and tip the mixture into the prepared tin.
7 Bake for 35–40 minutes, or until the cake springs back when lightly pressed.
8 Cool on a wire rack, whilst making the topping.

for the icing and assembly
1 Beat together the butter and cream cheese or mascarpone and gradually stir in the icing sugar and a teaspoon of the lemon juice.
2 If the mixture is still stiff, add a little more lemon juice and beat well until the icing is smooth.
3 Use a palette knife to spread the icing over the cooled cake, and use a fork to create a decorative pattern on the top.
4 Chill until required.

serving suggestions
Great at tea time or as a dessert after a light lunch or dinner.

storage
The cake can be refrigerated for 3–4 days, or frozen for up to 3 months. Defrost in the fridge.

allergens
Gluten (wheat), eggs, milk (butter/cream cheese), nuts (walnuts).

NUTRITION NOTE
Using rapeseed oil (which is usually used in the UK as vegetable oil), makes this sponge low in saturates and high in monounsaturates, so you can use butter and cream cheese in the icing without worrying you will have an overly rich cake.

desserts and baking

orange bran muffins

Whether for breakfast or a snack with a glass of milk or cup of herb tea, these easy-to-make muffins supply you with essential fibre, as well a small amount of iron and vitamin C. Make a batch and freeze — they defrost quickly so you can enjoy one at any time even when you have a fit of the midnight munchies.

serves 12
preparation time 10 minutes
cooking time 20 minutes

50 g All Bran
300 ml unsweetened orange juice
100 g raisins
2 medium eggs
50 g granulated sugar
50 ml vegetable oil
250 g self raising flour
1 tsp baking powder

1 Preheat the oven to 190°C, 170°C for fan oven or gas mark 5
2 Place 12 paper muffin cases in a muffin tray.
3 Soak the All Bran and raisins in the orange juice for 5 minutes whilst you prepare the remaining ingredients.
4 Whisk the eggs in a large bowl with the sugar and oil until combined.
5 Sieve the flour and baking powder together.
6 Pour the bran mixture into the egg mixture and beat well.
7 Fold in the flour to make a very thick batter.
8 Spoon the mixture into the muffin cases and bake for 20 minutes, or until the tops are springy to the touch.
9 Cool and serve as required.

serving suggestions
Eat with fresh sliced oranges and plain yogurt for a simple breakfast or with a glass of milk for a nourishing mid-morning snack.

storage
The muffins can be kept for 2 days in an airtight container, or frozen for up to 3 months.

allergens
Gluten (wheat), eggs.

chocolate Brazil brownies

Brazil nuts are one of the few good sources of the antioxidant selenium, which help protect you and your baby. If you are chocolate addict, eat one of these instead of a chocolate bar as they will provide you and your baby with more nutrients.

serves 12
preparation time 15 minutes
cooking time 30–35 minutes

75 g plain chocolate with at least 70% cocoa solids
75 g sunflower spread (not reduced fat)
150 g light muscovado sugar
1 tsp vanilla essence
2 medium eggs, beaten
100 g self raising flour
75 g Brazil nuts, roughly chopped

for the frosting
60 g plain chocolate with at least 70% cocoa solids
75 g icing sugar, sieved
1 tbsp water
½ teaspoon vanilla essence
25 g Brazil nuts, chopped.

1 Preheat the oven to 180°C, 160°C for fan oven or gas mark 4
2 Line an 20-cm square baking tin with greaseproof paper and oil lightly.
3 Place the chocolate and sunflower spread in a large heatproof bowl and melt over a pan of barely simmering water.
4 When melted, remove the bowl and beat in the eggs, sugar and vanilla.
5 Stir in the flour and nuts, and pour the batter into the prepared tin.
6 Bake for 30–35 minutes or until the brownies are just springy to the ouch. Cool.
7 To make the frosting, melt the chocolate in a small heatproof bowl over a pan of barely simmering water.
8 Stir in the icing sugar, vanilla essence and just enough water to make a thick but spreadable frosting.

9 Using a palette knife spread icing over the brownies, sprinkle over the Brazil nuts, and allow to set before cutting into 12 pieces.

serving suggestions
Delicious with a cup of tea, or have as a dessert with a scoop of vanilla ice cream.

storage
The brownies can be frozen for up to 3 months in an airtight container, or stored for a few days in a cool dry cupboard.

allergens
Wheat (gluten), eggs, nuts (Brazils).

desserts and baking

Cheddar and sundried tomato scones

Savoury scones make a welcome change to sandwiches or bread with a soup lunch. One scone provides a quarter of your day's calcium needs.

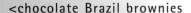

serves 8
preparation time 10 minutes
cooking time 15 minutes

---

150 g plain white flour
100 g wholemeal flour
3 tsps baking powder
80 g sundried tomatoes in oil, drained and roughly chopped
100 g reduced fat Cheddar cheese, grated
284 g carton buttermilk
a little milk as required

1 Preheat the oven to 210°C, 195°C for fan oven or gas mark 8. Grease a baking tray.
2 Sieve the 2 flours and baking powder into a mixing bowl, adding any bran which remains in the sieve.
3 Add the tomatoes and 75 g of the cheese.
4 Stir in the buttermilk to make a soft but not sticky dough. Add a little milk if it is too dry, or more flour if too sticky.

5 Pop the baking sheet into the oven to heat up whilst you prepare the dough.
6 Place the dough on a floury surface and lightly roll out to around 2 cm thickness. Using a round cutter, cut out 8 scones
7 Remove the hot baking sheet from the oven and place the scones on it.
8 Brush the top of each scone with a little milk and sprinkle over the remaining cheese.
9 Bake for 12–15 minutes, or until the scones are just golden brown.
10 Cool slightly and serve.

serving suggestions
Spread with low-fat soft cheese and eat with a piece of celery or use to accompany a bowl of soup.

storage
The scones are best on the day they are made, but can be frozen for up to 3 months. They will quickly defrost and can be reheated successfully in a microwave oven.

allergens
Gluten (wheat), milk (buttermilk and cheese).

<chocolate Brazil brownies

GRATING CHEESE
An upright grater is quick and easy to use, producing coarse shreds. A rotary grater may be better if you want the cheese to be finer. For the best results, grate cheese straight from the refrigerator.

desserts and baking

153

NUTRITIONAL ANALYSIS

Each recipe has been analysed on a single portion amount. Where a micronutrient is at least 25% of RNI (reference nutritional intake) during pregnancy, this has been indicated.

Almond rice: Energy 349 kcal; Protein 7.8 g; Carbohydrate 43.5g of which sugars 2.1 g; Fat 15.8g of which saturates 1.2g; Fibre 2.7g; Sodium 0.2g; Salt 0.5g.

Apple and blackcurrant oat crumble: Energy 300 kcal; Protein 4.6g; Carbohydrate 52.2g of which sugars 26.5g; Fat 10.5g of which saturates 2.3g; Fibre 7.3g; Sodium 0.1g; Salt 0.25g; Iron 5.1mg (34% RNI); Vitamin C 19.5mg (39% RNI).

Apple, sage and walnut sauce: Energy 90 kcal; Protein 1.5g; Carbohydrate 7.8g of which sugars 7.7g; Fat 6.1g of which saturates 0.5g; Fibre 1.5g; Sodium 0g; Salt 0g.

Asparagus risotto: (analysed with water and vermouth not stock). Energy 477 kcal; Protein 16.0g; Carbohydrate 61.1g of which sugars 5.7g; Fat 16.8g of which saturates 4.4g; Fibre 5.3g; Sodium 0.2g; Salt 0.5g; Calcium 212mg (30% RNI).

Baba ganoush with bread and asparagus tips: Energy 293 kcal; Protein 12.1g; Carbohydrate 32.5g of which sugars 4.8g; Fat 13g of which saturates 3.7g; Calcium 245mg (35% RNI); Iron 3.85mg (26% RNI); Zinc 2.35mg (34% RNI); Folate 96mcg (32% RNI).

Baked beef and sour cherries: Energy 374 kcal; Protein 30.4g; Carbohydrate 40.7g of which sugars 12.7g; Fat 7.3g of which saturates 1.9g; Fibre 2.2g; Sodium 0.1g; Salt 0.2g; Iron 3.72mg (25% RNI); Zinc 7.34mg (>100% RNI); Vitamin A 274mcg (40% RNI); Vitamin B$_3$ (niacin) 3.4mg (26% RNI); Vitamin B$_6$ 0.41 (34% RNI); Vitamin B$_{12}$ 2.5 mcg (166% RNI).

Baked figs with pistachios and honey yogurt: Energy 206 kcal; Protein 7.4g; Carbohydrate 26.65g of which sugars 26.2g; Fat 8.6g of which saturates 2.2g; Fibre 3.8g; Sodium 0.1g; Salt 0.2g Calcium 195mg (27% RNI).

Barley and roasted vegetable salad with pumpkin seeds: Energy 480 kcal; Protein 20.1g; Carbohydrate 64.4g of which sugars 14.5g; Fat 20.1g of which saturates 3.0g; Fibre 13.1g; Sodium 0.2g; Salt 0.6g; Vitamin C 30mg (60% RNI); Folate 80mcg (26% RNI); Vitamin A 560mcg (80% RNI); Iron 6.3mg (42% RNI); Magnesium 143mg (52% RNI).

Bean and salsa wrap: Energy 345 kcal; Protein 19.2g; Carbohydrate 52.4g of which sugars 4.5g; Fat 5.8g of which saturates 2.5g; Fibre 7.6g; Sodium 0.8g; Salt 2.0g; Calcium 360mg (50% RNI); Vitamin A 350mcg (50% RNI).

Beef and beet sandwich: Energy 450 kcal; Protein 29.7g; Carbohydrate 44.0g of which sugars 8.3g; Fat 18.6g of which saturates 5.1g; Fibre 7.9g; Sodium 0.7g; Salt 1.8g; Iron 4.5mg (30% RNI); Zinc 6.0 mg (85% RNI); Folate 92 mcg (30% RNI).

Beef in beer: Energy 323 kcal; Protein 28.0g; Carbohydrate 20.3g of which sugars 12.1g; Fat 12.7g of which saturates 3.2g; Fibre 4.9g; Sodium 0.15g; Salt 0.4g; Zinc 7.3 mg (100% RNI); Copper 0.43mg (36% RNI); Vitamin A 1560mcg (220% RNI).

Berry yogurt breakfast: Energy 226 kcal; Protein 12.5g; Carbohydrate 26.8g of which sugars 23.6g; Fat 8.4g of which saturates 1.0g; Fibre 6.3g; Sodium 0.10g; Salt 0.25g; Calcium 280mg (40% RNI); Vitamin C 55mg (100% RNI); Zinc 2.0mg (28% RNI); Vitamin E 6.0mg.

*B*lack eye bean, currant and fresh mint stew: Energy 276 kcal; Protein 12.9g; Carbohydrate 44.4g of which sugars 19.7g; Fat 7.1g of which saturates 1.0g; Fibre 6.1g; Sodium trace; Salt trace; Folate 137mcg (45% RNI); Vitamin B$_1$ (thiamin) 0.24mg (26% RNI); Iron 5.4mg (36% RNI); Phosphorus 232mg (42% RNI).

Blackberry sauce: Energy 60 kcal; Protein 0.5 g; Carbohydrate 10.6g of which sugars 10.6g; Fat 0.1g of which saturates 0g; Fibre 2.7g; Sodium 0g; Salt 0g.

Brazil nut burgers: Energy 406 kcal; Protein 10.5g; Carbohydrate 42.3g of which sugars 11.6g; Fat 22.8g of which saturates 5.0g; Fibre 3.9g; Sodium 0.5g; Salt 1.3g; Calcium 175mg (25% RNI); Selenium 69mcg (115% RNI).

Broccoli with almonds: Energy 228 kcal; Protein 8.3 g; Carbohydrate 4.5 g of which sugars 3.0 g; Fat 19.8 g of which saturates 1.6 g; Fibre 4.9g; Sodium 0g; Salt 0g; Calcium 260mg (RNI 37 mg); Vitamin C 63mg (125% RNI); Folate 110 mcg (36% RNI).

Butternut squash bake with halloumi and pomegranate: Energy 461 kcal; Protein 18.4g; Carbohydrate 55.3g of which sugars 26.7g; Fat 20.1g of which saturates 9g; Fibre 9.6g; Sodium 0.6g; Salt 1.5g; Magnesium 99mg (36% RNI); Folate 75mcg (25% RNI); Vitamin C 40mg (80% RNI); Vitamin A 2030 mcg (290% RNI).

Carrot tray bake ($^1/_{16}$ cake including icing). Energy 285 kcal; Protein 3.3g; Carbohydrate 29.1g of which sugars 20.1g; Fat 18.4g of which saturates 3.0g; Fibre 1.6g; Sodium 0g; Salt 0g; Vitamin A 230mcg (33% RNI); Vitamin E 3.2mg.

Casserole of duck and shallots with peaches: Energy 178 kcal; Protein 14.3g; Carbohydrate 8.9g of which sugars 8.9g; Fat 9.8g of which saturates 1.7g; Fibre 3.4g; Sodium 0.1g; Salt 0.2g; Zinc 2.62 mg (37% RNI); Copper 0.3 mg (25% RNI).

Cheddar and sundried tomato scones: Energy 175 kcal; Protein 8.9g; Carbohydrate 24.6g of which sugars 2.1g; Fat 5.0g of which saturates 1.4g; Fibre 2.3g; Sodium 0.1g; Salt 0.25g; Calcium 75mg (25% RNI).

Chinese beef and noodles: Energy 474 kcal; Protein 30.6g; Carbohydrate 67.2g of which sugars 4.6g; Fat 11.1g of which saturates 2.2g; Fibre 7.4g; Sodium 1.1g; Salt 2.7g; Iron 5.0mg (33% RNI); Zinc 4.6mg (65% RNI); Vitamin B$_3$ (niacin) 7.0mg (53% RNI); Vitamin B$_1$ (thiamin) 0.23mg (25% RNI).

Chinese pork with plums: Energy 374 kcal; Protein 35.3g; Carbohydrate 33.8g of which sugars 30.8g; Fat 12.0g of which saturates 2.5g; Fibre 5.1g; Sodium 0.1g; Salt 0.2g; Vitamin B$_1$ (thiamin) 1.0mg (111% RNI); Vitamin B$_6$ 0.67mg (55% RNI); Zinc 3.6mg (51% RNI).

Chicken with pine nuts and prunes: Energy 366 kcal; Protein 30g; Carbohydrate 25.1g of which sugars 24.2g; Fat 15.2g of which saturates 1.8g; Fibre 5.8g; Sodium 0.1g; Salt 0.3g; Iron 3.85mg (26% RNI); Potassium 1165mg (323% RNI); Vitamin E 2.7mg.

Chocolate and chilli chicken: (analysed without yogurt). Energy 265 kcal; Protein 23.1g; Carbo-hydrate 23.6g of which sugars 22.4g; Fat 7.5g of which saturates 1.6g; Fibre 3.3g; Sodium 0.17g; Salt 0.4g; Potassium 915mg (26% RNI 26); Zinc 2.3mg (33% RNI); Copper 0.36 mg (33% RNI).

Chocolate Brazil brownies: Energy 261 kcal; Protein 3.7g; Carbohydrate 32.7g of which sugars 26.4g; Fat 14.1g of which saturates 4.5g; Fibre 1.2g; Sodium 0.1g; Salt 0.2g; Selenium 23mcg (38% RNI).

Chocolate brioche pudding: Energy 280 kcal; Protein 12.2g; Carbohydrate 36.2g of which sugars 20.6g; Fat 10.9g of which saturates 5.3g; Fibre 4.5g; Sodium 0.2g; Salt 0.5g; Vitamin B$_{12}$ 1.3 mcg (86% RNI).

Chorizo and black eyed beans with giant cous cous: (folate data based on boiled dried beans). Energy 380 kcal; Protein 24.1g; Carbohydrate 44.9g of which sugars 5.5g; Fat 14.0g of which saturates 5. g; Fibre 11.4g; Sodium 0.4g; Salt 1.0g; Folate 150mcg (50% RNI); Vitamin A 700mcg (100% RNI).

Citrus salad bowl: Energy 70 kcal; Protein 1.7g; Carbohydrate 16g of which sugars 15.8g; Fat 0.4g of which saturates 0g;

154

Fibre 3.6g; Sodium 0g; Salt 0g; Vitamin C 80mg (160% RNI).

Cos, chicken and croûtons: Energy 390 kcal; Protein 20.6g; Carbohydrate 28.4g of which sugars 6.0g; Fat 21.6g of which saturates 3.8g; Fibre 6.9g; Sodium 0.3g; Salt 0.7g; Vitamin B_3 (niacin) 7.9mg (60% RNI); Folate 75mcg (25% RNI); Vitamin C 70mg (140% RNI).

Crab cakes with watercress and orange salad: Energy 484 kcal; Protein 18.6g; Carbohydrate 32.6g of which sugars 12.8g; Fat 31.7g of which saturates 3.9g; Fibre 6.5g; Sodium 0.4g; Salt 1.0 g; Calcium 175mg (25% RNI); Vitamin C 80mg (160% RNI); Iodine 120mcg (85% RNI); Omega 3 2.45g.

Crab linguine: Energy 514 kcal; Protein 26.8g; Carbohydrate 58.8g of which sugars 4.7g; Fat 17.1g of which saturates 2.3g; Fibre 5.1g; Sodium 0.3g; Salt 0.8g; Magnesium 104 mg (38% RNI); Iron 4.5mg (30% RNI); Folic acid 90mcg (30% RNI); Omega 3 1.83g; Iodine 164mcg (117% RNI).

Creamy vegetarian mince: Energy 236 kcal; Protein 16.8g; Carbohydrate 8.8g of which sugars 6.4g; Fat 15.4g of which saturates 2.6g; Fibre 7.8g; Sodium 0.4g; Salt 0.9g; Zinc 6.1mg (87% RNI); Vitamin C 16.0mg (32% RNI; Copper 0.3mg (25% RNI).

Curly kale with garlic cherry tomatoes: Energy 85 kcal; Protein 2.9 g; Carbohydrate 3.6g of which sugars 3.1g; Fat 6. g of which saturates 1.0g; Fibre 2.1g; Sodium trace; Salt trace; Vitamin A 374mcg (53% RNI); Vitamin C 43mg (85 RNI).

Dried fruit salad: Energy 187 kcal; Protein 3.1g; Carbohydrate 44.8g of which sugars 44.8g; Fat 0.8g of which saturates 0g; Fibre 7.4g; Sodium 0g; Salt 0g; Potassium 1020mg (29% RNI); Vitamin C 26.4mg (52% RNI).

Duck and oriental mushroom stir fry: Energy 295 kcal; Protein 25.5g; Carbohydrate 15.7g of which sugars 7.4g; Fat 13.5g of which saturates 2.8g; Fibre 2.9g;

Sodium 0.5g; Salt 1.1g; Iron 4.24mg (28% RNI); Phosphorus 283mg (51% RNI); Vitamin B_{12} 3.4mcg (>200% RNI); Vitamin C 32 (64% RNI).

Duck with cherry sauce and leek mash: Energy 616 kcal; Protein 50.7g; Carbohydrate 64.4g of which sugars 32.8g; Fat 18.8 g of which saturates 5.2g; Fibre 7.8g; Sodium 0.4g; Salt 1.0g; Vitamin B_1 (thiamin) 0.4mg (43% RNI); Vitamin C 22.3mg (44% RNI).

Egg, tomato and onion roll: Energy 300 kcal; Protein 16.1g; Carbohydrate 43.3g of which sugars 6.6g; Fat 8.7g of which saturates 2.3g; Fibre 5.6g; Sodium 0.7g; Salt 1.8g; Calcium 234mg (33% RNI); Zinc 1.8mg (26% RNI); Folic acid 124mcg (41% RNI).

Fruity flapjack: (per 1/16 portion) Energy 200 kcal; Protein 3.3g; Carbohydrate 25.8g of which sugars 15.6g; Fat 10.0g of which saturates 2.2g; Fibre 3.0g; Sodium 0g; Salt 0g; Zinc 1.1mg; Iron 1.56 mg.

Ginger and orange slaw: Energy 60 kcal; Protein 1.5g; Carbohydrate 13.9g of which sugars 13.5g; Fat 0.3g of which saturates 0g; Fibre 3.6g; Sodium 0 g; Salt 0g; Vitamin A 560mcg (80% RNI); Vitamin C 60mg (120% RNI).

Gratin of potato: Energy 196 kcal; Protein 8.8g; Carbohydrate 28.9g of which sugars 4.4g; Fat 5.9g of which saturates 3.5g; Fibre 2.5g; Sodium 0.2g; Salt 0.5g; Calcium 190mg (27% RNI).

Greek style tomato and haddock: Energy 235 kcal; Protein 25.2g; Carbohydrate 6.3g of which sugars 6.2g; Fat 12.3g of which saturates 1.9g; Fibre 2.7g; Sodium 0.1g; Salt 0.25g; Iodine 316mcg (225% RNI); Vitamin C 17.3mg (34% RNI); Vitamin B_3 (niacin) 4.5mg (35% RNI).

Green beans and chorizo: Energy 220 kcal; Protein 10.6g; Carbohydrate 4.8g of which sugars 4.2g; Fat 17.7g of which saturates 5.7g; Fibre 3.4g; Sodium 0.4g; Salt 0g; Zinc 1.77mg (25% RNI); Vitamin C 15.5 (31% RNI); Vitamin B_1 (thiamin) 0.37 (41% RNI); Vitamin B_{12} 1.0 (66% RNI).

Green chilli edamame: Energy 111 kcal; Protein 6.8g; Carbohydrate 7.0g of which sugars 1.4g; Fat 6.3g of which saturates 0.8g; Fibre 5.6g; Sodium 0g; Salt 0g; Vitamin C 30 mg (60% RNI).

Herbed barley: Energy 190 kcal; Protein 5.7g; Carbohydrate 42.0g of which sugars 0.2g; Fat 1.1g of which saturates 0.1g; Fibre 8.0g; Sodium 0.2g; Salt 0.5g.

Home-made fish goujons with piquant avocado dip: Energy 370 kcal; Protein 33.3g; Carbohydrate 13.3g of which sugars 2.8g; Fat 20.8g of which saturates 7.2g; Fibre 3.6g; Sodium 0.4g; Salt 1.1g; Calcium 185mg (26% RNI); Magnesium 68mg (25% RNI); Vitamin B_2 (riboflavin) 0.46mg (33% RNI); Vitamin B_{12} 0.86mcg (57% RNI).

Honey-roasted stone fruit: Energy 112 kcal; Protein 1.8g; Carbohydrate 27.7g of which sugars 27.7g; Fat 0.2g of which saturates 0g; Fibre 3.8g; Sodium 0g; Salt .0g; Vitamin C 13.5g (27% RNI).

Hot potato salad: Energy 218 kcal; Protein 2.9g; Carbohydrate 27.5g of which sugars 2.2g; Fat 11.6g of which saturates 1.7 ; Fibre 3.3g; Sodium 0g; Salt 0g; Vitamin C 30.0mg (60% RNI).

Hungarian goulash: Energy 265 kcal; Protein 28.6g; Carbohydrate 15.3g of which sugars 9.8 Fat 10.3g of which saturates 3.1g; Fibre 3.8g; Sodium 0.2g; Salt 0.5g; Zinc 7.2mg (100% RNI); Vitamin A 675 mcg (90% RNI).

Italian chicken gnocchi: Energy 465 kcal; Protein 27.3g; Carbohydrate 72.0g of which sugars 11.3g; Fat 9.6g of which saturates 1.6g; Fibre 10.4g; Sodium 0.3g; Salt 0.8g; Iron 4.6mg (31% RNI); Vitamin C 28mg (56% RNI 56); Folate 90mcg (30% RNI).

Jambalaya: Energy 520 kcal; Protein 35.7g; Carbohydrate 72.5g of which sugars 6.1g; Fat 11.7g of which saturates 4.2g; Fibre 3.2g; Sodium 1.0g; Salt 2.5g; Vitamin B_1 (thiamin) 0.4mg (44% RNI); Vitamin B_3 (niacin) 3.57mg (27% RNI); Vitamin B_{12} 4.5mcg (300% RNI).

Kachumbari: Energy 23 kcal; Protein 1.0g; Carbohydrate 4.3g of which sugars 3.8g; Fat 0.3g of which saturates 0.1g; Fibre 1.7g; Sodium 0.1g; Salt 0.25g; Vitamin C 41mg (82% RNI).

Lamb and pepper koftas with tzatziki: Energy 353 kcal; Protein 29.1g; Carbohydrate 16.4g of which sugars 9.2g; Fat 19.6g of which saturates 7.2g; Fibre 3.7g; Sodium 0.3g; Salt 0.8g; Vitamin B_{12} 2.0mcg (133% RNI); Vitamin C 50mg (100% RNI); Zinc 4.0mg (57% RNI).

Mango and lime dessert: Energy 150 kcal; Protein 8.1g; Carbohydrate 21.8g of which sugars 21.0g; Fat 4.0g of which saturates 0.6g; Fibre 5.6g; Sodium 0g; Salt 0g; Calcium 464mg (66% RNI); Vitamin A 175mcg (25% RNI); Vitamin C 57mg (114% RNI).

Mediterranean vegetable parcels: Energy 270 kcal; Protein 9.2g; Carbohydrate 26.6g of which sugars 5.5g; Fat 14.2g pf which saturates 4.2g; Fibre 1.9g; Sodium 0.6g; Salt 1.4g; Vitamin C 25 mg (50% RNI).

Mexican brunch: (analysis with wholemeal tortilla). Energy 387 kcal; Protein 18.9g; Carbohydrate 59.9g of which sugars 14.9g; Fat 10.0g of which saturates 2.6g; Fibre 9.4g; Sodium 0.3g; Salt 0.7g; Iron 4.5mg (27% RNI); Vitamin C 15.3mg (30% RNI); Folate 100mcg (33% RNI).

Moroccan hummus with flatbread: (with 1 wholemeal pitta*). Energy 172 kcal (376 kcal*); Protein 5.9g(14.9g*); Carbohydrate 10.0g of which sugars 0.5g (49.3g of which sugars 3.0g*); Fat 12.4g of which saturates 1.7g (14.7g* of which saturates 2.1g*); Fibre 3.6g (7.8g*); Sodium 0.2g (0.7 g*); Salt 0.6g (1.7g*); Iron 4.0mg (27mg*); Zinc 2.46 mg (35 mg*).

Moroccan lamb tagine: Energy 333 kcal; Protein 25.4g; Carbohydrate 17.8g of which sugars 16.3g; Fat 18.7g of which saturates 7.8g; Fibre 4.5g; Sodium 0.1g; Salt 0.2g; Iron 4.2mg (28% RNI); Zinc 5.3 mg (75% RNI); Vitamin B_{12} 2.33mcg (150% RNI).

Mozzarella turkey with fig and ginger 'jam': Energy 278 kcal; Protein 33.8g; Carbohydrate 7.1g of which sugars 6.6g; Fat 12.8g of which saturates 6.8g; Fibre 2.0g; Sodium 0.2g; Salt 0.5g; Calcium 190mg (27% RNI); Vitamin B_3 (niacin) 6.5mg (50% RNI); Vitamin B_{12} 1.7mcg (110% RNI).

Mushroom and asparagus omelette: Energy 297 kcal; Protein 21.6g; Carbohydrate 2.3g of which sugars 2.0g; Fat 23.2g of which saturates 4.7g; Fibre 3.1g; Sodium 0.2g; Salt 0.5g; Iron 3.7mg (25% RNI); Zinc 2.8mg (40% RNI); Vitamin D 2.5mcg (25% RNI); Folate 138mcg (46% RNI); Iodine 76mcg (108% RNI).

Mushroom stuffed chicken with puy lentils: Energy 263 kcal; Protein 30g; Carbohydrate 19.9g of which sugars 1.6g; Fat 7.6g pf which saturates 1.4g; Fibre 4.1g; Sodium 0.5g; Salt 1.25g; Iron 5.0mg (35% RNI); Copper 0.6mg (50% RNI); Zinc 3.00mg (42% RNI).

Paella: Energy 455 kcal; Protein 33.4g; Carbohydrate 58.7g of which sugars 7.8g; Fat 9.1g of which saturates 1.4g; Fibre 6.2g; Sodium 0.4g; Salt 1.0g; Zinc 2.9mg (41% RNI); Vitamin C 45mg (90% RNI); Vitamin A 460mcg (65% RNI).

Orange and mint cous cous: (based on regular [not wholegrain] cous cous). Energy 142 kcal; Protein 3.4g; Carbohydrate 32.5g of which sugars 6.6g; Fat 0.6g of which saturates 0g; Fibre 2.6g; Sodium 0g; Salt 0g; Vitamin C 25.0mg (50% RNI).

Orange and pomegranate salad: Energy 115 kcal; Protein 2.6g; Carbohydrate 27.3g of which sugars 27.1g; Fat 0.3 g of which saturates 0g; Fibre 4.1g; Sodium 0g; Salt 0g; Folic acid 75mcg (25% RNI); Vitamin C 94mg (188% RNI).

Orange bran muffins: Energy 178 kcal; Protein 3.9g; Carbohydrate 29.9g of which sugars 13.1g; Fat 5.6g pf which saturates 0.6g; Fibre 2.4g; Sodium 0.1 g; Salt 0.2 g.

Pasta primavera: Energy 435 kcal; Protein 18.7g; Carbohydrate 67.6g of which sugars 6.1g; Fat 11.7g of which saturates 4.1g; Fibre 14.4g; Sodium 0.1g; Salt 0.3g; Iron 5.0 mg (34% RNI); Vitamin C 25.1mg (50% RNI); Vitamin B_3 (niacin) 3.5mg (27% RNI).

Patatas bravas: Energy 236 kcal; Protein 5.8g; Carbohydrate 35.6g of which sugars 7.3g; Fat 9.1g of which saturates 0.8g; Fibre 5.2g; Sodium 0.1g; Salt 0.2g; Vitamin B_6 0.55 mg (45% RNI); Vitamin A 218mcg (31% RNI); Vitamin C 22.7mg (45% RNI).

Peanut satay sauce: Energy 142 kcal; Protein 5.5g; Carbohydrate 2.4g of which sugars 1.6g; Fat 12.4g of which saturates 3.4g; Fibre 1.6g; Sodium 0.3g; Salt 0.75g.

Pears in chocolate sauce: Energy 300 kcal; Protein 2.8g; Carbohydrate 49.9g of which sugars 49.9g; Fat 11.4g of which saturates 7.0g; Fibre 5.0g; Sodium 0g; Salt 0g.

Pork and roasted vegetable tray bake: Energy 444 kcal; Protein 24.7g; Carbohydrate 39.9g of which sugars 12.8g; Fat 21.8g of which saturates 5.4g; Fibre 5.5g; Sodium 0.2g; Salt 0.4g; Vitamin B_1 (thiamin) 0.8mg (90% RNI); Vitamin C 50mg (100% RNI); Vitamin A 900mcg (125% RNI).

Pork with pineapple: Energy 357 kcal; Protein 34.8g; Carbohydrate 29.1g of which sugars 27.1g; Fat 12.2g of which saturates 2.5g; Fibre 4.5g; Sodium 0.1g Salt 0.25g; Vitamin B_1 (thiamin) 1.0mg (115% RNI); Vitamin B_3 (niacin) 6.9mg (53% RNI).

Potato-topped creamy fish pie: Energy 406 kcal; Protein 36g; Carbohydrate 44.5g of which sugars 8.5g; Fat 10.6g of which saturates 3.8g; Fibre 4.4g; Sodium 0.8g; Salt 2.0g; Calcium 233mg (33% RNI); Vitamin B_3 (niacin) 7.2mg (55% RNI); Magnesium 90mg (33% RNI).

Pot roasted chicken: Energy 513 kcal; Protein 38.9g; Carbohydrate 34.4g of which sugars 9.4g; Fat 25.5g of which saturates 6.6g; Fibre 8.1g; Sodium 0.5g; Salt 1.3g; Vitamin B_3 (niacin) 7.18mg (55% RNI); Folate 119mcg (39% RNI); Zinc 2.84mg (40% RNI); Vitamin A 719mcg (100% RNI).

Pot roasted lamb shanks: Energy 340 kcal; Protein 32.00g; Carbohydrate 19.5g of which sugars 11.2g; Fat 14.9g of which saturates 4.6g; Fibre 3.9g; Sodium 0.1 g; Salt 0.3g; Iron 3.76mg (25% RNI); Zinc 4.94mg (70% RNI); Vitamin A 1415 mcg (>200% RNI); Vitamin B_3 (niacin) 3.7mcg (28% RNI).

Quinoa and sunflower seeds: Energy 260 kcal; Protein 9.9g; Carbohydrate 35.0g of which sugars 3.7g; Fat 10.0g of which saturates 1.2g; Fibre 0.9g; Sodium 0.1g; Salt 0.3g; Iron 5.2mg (35% RNI); Zinc 2.4mg (34% RNI); Vitamin E 3.2mg.

Quinoa, feta and spinach salad: Energy 386 kcal; Protein 18.9g; Carbohydrate 35.9g of which sugars 5.8g; Fat 19.5g of which saturates 7.3g; Fibre 1.5g; Sodium 0.8g; Salt 2.0g; Calcium 290mg (41% RNI); Iron 5.9mg (40% RNI); Zinc 2.8mg (40% RNI); Vitamin B_3 (niacin) 3.2mg (25% RNI); Vitamin C 20.0mg (40% RNI); Vitamin A 475mcg (67% RNI).

Raisin and apple pancakes: (2 pancakes and 1 tbsp 3% fat plain yogurt). Energy 410 kcal; Protein 14.9g; Carbohydrate 71.3g of which sugars 26.9g; Fat 9.2 g of which saturates 2.4g; Fibre 6.2g; Sodium 0.1g; Salt 0.3g; Calcium 235mg (33% RNI); Magnesium 69mg (25% RNI); Zinc 2.45mg (35% RNI); Vitamin B_3 (niacin) 3.4mg (26% RNI).

Raspberry and pomegranate jelly: (based on using xylitol and regular [not sugar-free] syrup). Energy 73 kcal; Protein 3.3g; Carbohydrate 18.1g of which sugars 10.7g; Fat 0.2g of which saturates 0 g; Fibre 2.8g; Sodium 0 g; Salt 0 g; Vitamin C 38mg (76% RNI).

Raspberry porridge with walnuts: Energy 380 kcal; Protein 14.8g; Carbohydrate 50.0g of which sugars 23.0g; Fat 14.9g of which saturates 4.0g; Fibre 6.8g; Sodium 0.1g; Salt 0.2g; Calcium 350mg (50% RNI); Vitamin B_3 (niacin) 3.4mg (26% RNI); Magnesium 96mg (35% RNI).

Ratatouille with halloumi and bread: Energy 450 kcal; Protein 21.5g; Carbohydrate 42.6g of which sugars 10.2g; Fat 22.4g of which saturates 11.5g; Fibre 4.9g; Sodium 964g; Salt 2.4g; Vitamin C 45mg (90% RNI); Vitamin A 280mcg (40% RNI).

Roast beet and butternut squash: Energy 136 kcal; Protein 2.7g; Carbohydrate 15.6g of which sugars 11.2g; Fat 7.5g of which saturates 1.0g; Fibre 3.9 g; Sodium trace; Salt trace; Folate 75mcg (25% RNI); Vitamin A 500mcg (72 RNI).

Roasted baby vegetables with tofu: (based on 3 portions). Energy 193 kcal; Protein 10.6g; Carbohydrate 10.6g of which sugars 8.7g; Fat 12.3g of which

saturates 1.7g; Fibre 4.5g; Sodium 0.1g; Salt 0.3g; Calcium 544mg (77% RNI); Vitamin C 46 (76% RNI).

Roasted pepper and olive bruschetta: Energy 172 kcal; Protein 3.1g; Carbohydrate 17.5g of which sugars 4.1g; Fat 10.5g of which saturates 1.7g; Fibre 2.9g; Sodium 0.5g; Salt 2.5g; Vitamin A 577mcg 100% RNI).

Roasted red pepper pâté: Energy 200 kcal; Protein 2.0g; Carbohydrate 7.4g of which sugars 6.5g; Fat 18.1g of which saturates 8.1g; Fibre 2.2g; Sodium 0.01g; Salt 0.1g; Vitamin A 575mcg (82% RNI); Vitamin C 62.2mg (120% RNI).

Salmon and asparagus en croûte: Energy 413 kcal; Protein 25.8g; Carbohydrate 26.2g of which sugars 3.3g; Fat 22.7g of which saturates 3.4g; Fibre 1.5g; Sodium 0.3g; Salt 0.8g; Vitamin D 4.6mcg (46% RNI); Omega 3 3.9g.

Sardine and cheese toastie: Energy 425 kcal; Protein 29.5g; Carbohydrate 47.9g of which sugars 6.1g; Fat 14.0g of which saturates 4.6g; Fibre 4.7g; Sodium 0.8g; Salt 2.1g; Calcium 650 mg (92% RNI); Iron 3.7mg (25% RNI); Zinc 2.8mg (40% RNI); Vitamin B_{12} 9.3 mcg (620% RNI); Vitamin D 3.0mcg (30% RNI).

Sardine and pepper strudels: Energy 325 kcal; Protein 17.5g; Carbohydrate 31.4g of which sugars 5.8g; Fat 14.5g of which saturates 2.2g; Fibre 1.9g; Sodium 0.5g; Salt 1.25g; Calcium 258mg (36% RNI); Vitamin C 30mg (60% RNI); Vitamin D 2.5mcg (25% RNI); Vitamin B_{12} 7.5mg (500% RNI).

Sausage and orzo hotpot: Energy 585 kcal; Protein 24.7g; Carbohydrate 67.8g of which sugars 14.4g; Fat 26.0g of which saturates 7.4g; Fibre 7.2g; Sodium 0.9g; Salt 2.25g; Iron 4.0 mg (27% RNI); Vitamin C 25mg (50% RNI); Vitamin A 811mcg (115% RNI).

Sea bass with pomegranate salsa: Energy 226 kcal; Protein 27.1g; Carbohydrate 9.8g of which sugars 9.3g; Fat 9.0g of which saturates 1.4g; Fibre 1.8g; Sodium trace; Salt trace; Vitamin B_3 (niacin) 5.0mg (38% RNI); Calcium 186mg (26% RNI).

Sesame and coriander chicken with mango salsa: Energy 308 kcal; Protein 36.3g; Carbohydrate 10.9g of which sugars 9.7g; Fat 14.6g of which saturates 2.8g;

Fibre 5.6g; Sodium 0.15g; Salt 0.4 g; Zinc 3.5mg (50% RNI); Vitamin C 59mg (115% RNI); Vitamin B$_3$ (niacin) 6.37mg (50% RNI); Vitamin B$_{12}$ 1.6mcg (105% RNI).

Smoked mackerel, ricotta and beetroot bruschetta: Energy 209 kcal; Protein 8.9g; Carbohydrate 15.9g of which sugars 2.6g; Fat 12.6g of which saturates 3.4g; Fibre 1.1g; Sodium 0.38g; Salt 1.0g; Iodine 38mcg (27% RNI); Vitamin D 1.72mcg (17% RNI); Vitamin B$_{12}$ 1.55mcg (100% RNI); Omega 3 1.4g.

Smoked salmon flakes with herbed lentils: Energy 305 kcal; Protein 33.1g; Carbohydrate 23.6g of which sugars 2.7g; Fat 9.3g of which saturates 3.5g; Fibre 7.3g; Sodium 0.5g; Salt 1.3g; Iron 5.33mg (35% RNI); Omega 3 2.8g; Zinc 2.3mg (33% RNI); Vitamin D 3.7mcg estimated (37% RNI).

Spinach stuffed chicken breasts with proscuitto: Energy 313 kcal; Protein 40.2g; Carbohydrate 0.3g of which sugars 0.2g; Fat 17.0g of which saturates 6.8g; Fibre 1.0g; Sodium 0.7g; Salt 1.8g; Vitamin A 314mcg (44% RNI); Vitamin B$_3$ (niacin) 8.5mg (65% RNI).

Spinach with currants and pine nuts: Energy 240 kcal; Protein 4.4g; Carbohydrate 18.2g of which sugars 18.1g; Fat 17.3g of which saturates 1.7g; Fibre 3.9g; Sodium trace; Salt trace; Vitamin A 770mcg (110% RNI); Vitamin E 3.6mg.

Sprats with avocado and cherry tomatoes: Energy 527 kcal; Protein 24.0g; Carbohydrate 3.9g of which sugars 2.8g; Fat 46.0g of which saturates 8.3g; Fibre 4.6g; Sodium 0.2g; Salt 0.5g; Iodine 75mcg (106% RNI); Vitamin C 25mg (50% RNI); Omega 3 3.42g; Vitamin D 20mcg (200% RNI).

Steak and broccoli with noodles: Energy 416 kcal; Protein 35.4g; Carbohydrate 30.1g of which sugars 6.6g; Fat 17.7g of which saturates 3.2g; Fibre 5.7g; Sodium 0.5g; Salt 1.3g; Iron 4.2mg (28% RNI); Vitamin C 35mg (70% RNI); Vitamin B$_{12}$ 2.2mcg (150% RNI).

Strawberry mousse: Energy 127 kcal; Protein 8.4g; Carbohydrate 24.2g of which sugars 24.2g; Fat 0.3g of which saturates 0.1g; Fibre 2.3g; Sodium 0g; Salt 0g; Vitamin C 70mg (140% RNI).

Stuffed Portobello mushrooms: Energy 325 kcal; Protein 18.9g; Carbohydrate 22.3g of which sugars 1.7g; Fat 18.4g of which saturates 3.3g; Fibre 5.2g; Sodium 0.4g; Salt 1.1g; Calcium 313g (44% RNI); Vitamin B$_2$ (riboflavin) 0.36mg (25% RNI); Vitamin B$_3$ (niacin) 3.73mg (28% RNI); Vitamin B$_{12}$ 0.39mcg (26% RNI).

Summer fruit compote: (values given for sugar; those for xylitol in parenthesis). Energy 147 kcal (109); Protein 1.9g (1.9g) Carbohydrate 36.4g (35.2g) of which sugars 36.4g (10.2g); Fat 0.3g (0.3g) of which saturates 0g (0g); Fibre 10.4g (10.4g); Sodium 0g (0g); Salt 0g (0g); (Vitamin C 62.2mg (62.2mg) (125% RNI).

Sweet potato and chestnut jalousie: (based on ⅙ portion). Energy 556 kcal; Protein 6.6g; Carbohydrate 64.7g of which sugars 13.7g; Fat 30.1g of which saturates 15.2g; Fibre 9.9g; Sodium 0.4g; Salt 1.0g; Vitamin A 1171mcg (170% RNI); Copper 0.65mg (54% RNI).

Tabbouleh with pine nuts: Energy 313 kcal; Protein 8.3g; Carbohydrate 30g of which sugars 4.2g; Fat 18.3g of which saturates 2.2g; Fibre 6.8 g; Sodium trace; Salt trace; Magnesium 12mg (47% RNI); Iron 4.5mg (32% RNI); Zinc 1.9mg (27% RNI); Vitamin C 19.6mg (39% RNI).

Tarka dhal: Energy 304 kcal; Protein 18.9g; Carbohydrate 45.7g of which sugars 3.9g; Fat 7.0 g of which saturates 0.6g; Fibre 9.7g; Sodium 0.13g; Salt 0.3g; Iron 6.9mg (46% RNI); Zinc 2.5mg (36% RNI).

Tarragon sauce: Energy 61 kcal; Protein 1.1g; Carbohydrate 2.4g of which sugars 1.0g; Fat 5.2g of which saturates 1.8g; Fibre 0.3g; Sodium 0g; Salt 0.1 g.

Teriyaki turkey with sesame cucumber salad: Energy 296 kcal; Protein 13.1g; Carbohydrate 5.2g of which sugars 4.1g; Fat 15.6g of which saturates 1.6g; Fibre 2.0g; Sodium 0.5g; Salt 1.5g; Vitamin B$_3$ (niacin) 8.3mg (86% RNI; Vitamin E 2.6mg.

Tomato, basil and mozzarella bruschetta: Energy 197 kcal; Protein 7.5g; Carbohydrate16.6g of which sugars 3.1g; Fat 11.7g of which saturates 4.7g; Fibre 2.0g; Sodium 0.26g; Salt 0.6g; Vitamin C 15.3mg (30% RNI).

Traditional rice pudding: Energy 158 kcal; Protein 7.5g; Carbohydrate 28.1g of which sugars 9.4g; Fat 3.3g of which saturates 1.9g; Fibre 0.5g; Sodium 0.1g; Salt 0.1g; Calcium 228mg (32% RNI).

Tuna and vegetable pasta bake: Energy 450 kcal; Protein 32.4g; Carbohydrate 34.1g of which sugars 9.2g; Fat 21.8g of which saturates 7.1g; Fibre 4.0g; Sodium 0.4g; Salt 1.0g; Calcium 250mg (35% RNI); Vitamin C 50mg (100% RNI); Iodine 52mcg (38% RNI); Vitamin B$_{12}$ 3.6mcg (240% RNI).

Tuna steaks with sundried tomato crust and lime dressing: Energy 407 kcal; Protein 45.4g; Carbohydrate 14.0g of which sugars 2.9g; Fat 19.3g of which saturates 5.1g; Fibre 1.9g; Sodium 0.2g; Salt 0.5g; Vitamin D 12.3mcg (125% RNI); Omega 3 2.24g.

Turkey herb burgers with fruity salsa: (48g wholemeal roll with olive spread, ⅓ recipe salsa and 30g watercress). Energy 343 kcal; Protein 25.8g; Carbohydrate 31.8g of which sugars 10.4g; Fat 13.5g of which saturates 2.3g; Fibre 34.4g; Sodium 0.4g; Salt 1.1g; Zinc 2.86mg (40% RNI); Selenium 15mcg (25% RNI); Vitamin B$_1$ (thiamin) 0.26mg (25% RNI); Vitamin B$_3$ (niacin) 6.25mg (48% RNI) Vitamin C 32.3mg (64% RNI).

Two pear salad: Energy 310 kcal; Protein 2.2g; Carbohydrate 19.8g of which sugars 18.8g; Fat 25.5g of which saturates 4.1g; Fibre 6.5g; Sodium 0g; Salt 0g; Vitamin E 3.9mg.

Tzatziki with raw vegetables: Energy 123 kcal; Protein 9.4g; Carbohydrate 7.6g of which sugars 6.8g; Fat g 6.2g of which saturates 1.0g; Fibre 2.9g; Sodium 0.2g; Salt 0.6g; Vitamin A 181mcg (25% RNI); Folate 75mcg (25% RNI); Vitamin C 29 (58% RNI).

Vegetable pancakes with red pepper sauce: (based on 2 small pancakes plus ¼ recipe of vegetables and sauce). Energy 489 kcal; Protein 24.1g; Carbohydrate 48.9g of which sugars 14.6g; Fat 23.3g of which saturates 5.4g; Fibre 10.5g; Sodium 0.3g; Salt 0.7g; Calcium 420 mg (60% RNI); Zinc 2.7 mg (38% RNI); Vitamin A 1050 mcg (15% RNI); Vitamin C 45.7mg (90% RNI); Vitamin B$_6$ 0.53 mg (44% RNI); Folate 100mcg (33% RNI).

Water chestnut and cashew nut stir fry: Energy 384 kcal; Protein 12.2g; Carbohydrate 36.4g of which sugars 10.1g; Fat 21.1g of which saturates 3.3g; Fibre 6.8g; Sodium 0.23g; Salt 0.6g; Vitamin A 337mcg (48% RNI); Vitamin C 43.0mg (86% RNI); Iron 3.9mg (26% RNI).

Watercress and salmon salad: Energy 320 kcal; Protein 25.6g; Carbohydrate 5.4g of which sugars 4.8g; Fat 21.7g of which saturates 7.7g; Fibre 1.6g; Sodium 0.2g; Salt 0.5g; Vitamin D 5.5mcg (55% RNI); Vitamin A 210 mcg (299% RNI); Omega 3 2.7g.

Wild mushroom and rosemary sauce: Energy 59 kcal; Protein 1.6g; Carbohydrate 3.6g of which sugars 0.3g; Fat 4.3g of which saturates 0.8g; Fibre 0.9g; Sodium 0.1g; Salt 0.2g.

Wild rice pilaff with haddock, peas and capers: Energy 448 kcal; Protein 34.4g; Carbohydrate 63.2g of which sugars 3.3g; Fat 8.3g of which saturates 1.0g; Fibre 6.1g; Sodium 0.4g; Salt 1.0g; Zinc 3.5mg (50% RNI); Vitamin B$_3$ (niacin) 6.5mg (50% RNI); Vitamin B$_{12}$1.25mcg (80% RNI).

INDEX

ACKNOWLEDGEMENTS

I'd like to acknowledge the work of Amy Carroll and Chrissie Lloyd who waited patiently as this new edition evolved. Also my family who have eaten every recipe in the book more than once, and who are my most reliable critics.